8⁹⁵

9-4-82
From Jane to "

Voices of Kensington

VANISHING MILLS
VANISHING NEIGHBORHOODS

by Jean Seder

Photographs by Nancy Hellebrand

WHITMORE PUBLISHING COMPANY
35 Cricket Terrace • *Ardmore, Pennsylvania*

I would like to thank all those who contributed to this book: those who allowed me to use their names, those who asked that I use pseudonyms, and those who so graciously consented to interviews but whose stories could not be used because of space limitations: John Samanac, *Master Warper,* Howard Davenport, *Warehouse Manager,* and Guy Coville, *Textile Magazine Filler.*

Photo Credits:
Nancy Hellebrand is a full-time photographer and photography teacher. Her book, *Londoners,* 1974, is distributed by Light Impressions. Her work is in museum collections in London and New York. She lives in Philadelphia. (Photographs other than Ms. Hellebrand's, on pages 6, 9, 10, 12 and 13, are in the public domain.)

Copyright © 1982 by Jean Seder
All Rights Reserved
ISBN 87426-055-8
Library of Congress Catalog Card No.: 82-2691
Printed in the United States of America

To the People of Kensington

Contents

Foreword   vii

Jean Seder: *Author and Fellow Worker*   1

MOTHER AND SON
Irene Brown: *Early Kensington Resident*   5
Tom Brown: *Plant Manager*   8

Gus Misuinas: *Hosiery Spinner*   12

Catherine Hutt: *Mother*   15

Arthur Adams: *Textile Card Cutter*   18

Joe Barker: *Textile Weaver—Loom Fixer*   21

DUO
Marion Knuttel: *Textile Winder*   26
Joe Knuttel: *Textile Weaver—Loom Fixer*   30

Matt Pytel: *Textile Weaver—Loom Fixer*   34

Irene (Rocky) Dougherty: *Textile Winder—Loom Magazine Filler*   36

Samuel Berg: *Shoemaker*   41

Lena Sandberg: *Meat Store Manager*   46

William Hartley: *Carpet Weaver—Piano Player in Silent Movies*   50

TRIO
"Aunt Sadie": *Textile Burler and Mender*   57
Nancy McCoy: *Forelady of a Textile Burling and Mending Room*   64
Betty Makarewicz: *Textile Burler and Mender*   72

John Sullivan: *Teacher—Writer—Educator*   80

Foreword

Most of those who speak here are workers
in the mills of Kensington.
A few are shopkeepers serving them.
Everything they tell you is true.
They speak from their hearts.
They remember mostly the good times.
They talk about their social life, their families.
Not too much about working.
The hard times and the ugliness you have to
read between the lines, although the women
speak more freely than the men.

To tell the story of Kensington is to tell of vanishing mills.
Vanishing mills. Vanishing neighborhoods.
Simple pleasures of living close to your neighbors
gone forever, except held still in the hearts
of these tenacious few.

> *After my husband died, and I was alone*
> *with the children still young, I remember*
> *how good my neighbors were.*
> *Many the night Mrs. McGuinnis next door*
> *would come over with a hot platter—*
> *so good she was.*

From the beginning, Kensington was a place where
you could make a living no matter what your craft.
There was this promise of steady work for all,
and to it came the poor of Europe used to working with their hands.
They came, went to work at their accustomed trades,
settled down with relatives and friends and
created their own neighborhoods.

Once settled they almost never moved away,
not even when the mills shut down during the depression.

> *I sold soap from door to door, and played*
> *the organ at the Eagle Theater. The wife*
> *worked at the Quaker Lace Company.*
> *They was working a few days most weeks*
> *because one thing folks did around here*
> *was hang lace curtains at their front windows,*
> *and wash their front steps down every Saturday.*

They worked, all of them, starting early in their lives,
long hours for little pay. But mostly they talk of
friends, children, parents.
The women tell how they worked together to raise
children without men. How the mother would
work the third shift, midnight to seven,
and her daughter would work the second shift,
three-thirty to twelve. Between them
they took care of their children.

> *Someone was always there with me.*
> *I never felt like I was alone.*

They remember the games of their childhoods,
talk of social life in the taprooms, block parties,
the long walks they took together on the avenue.

A common thread runs throughout. They all believe
in working hard for what you get. Proud of their
backgrounds and close to their families, they take care
of parents and those children that are too sick
in mind or body to leave them. They keep them at home
and manage somehow for their care.
They look back on childhoods that were wild and free
and self-sufficient. They left school early
and went to work with no regrets.

> *My parents told me I'd be sorry.*
> *I never was.*

Most, except for those in their eighties,
are still working. The oldsters would like to be.

Work is their life, their independence.
They had no time for hobbies.

> *My sister is mad these days because they*
> *retired her. A lot of people don't like that—*
> *being retired.*

Everything they tell you is what they remember about
their lives, their work. But the scene they remember
no longer exists. Kensington today is a passed-over,
deteriorated, forgotten section of industrial Philadelphia.
Almost all the mills have gone. They've moved South,
or gone out of business. Periodically the children
set fire to the empty shells of factories,
and the city levels the ruins into another empty lot.

Bewildered at the changes, these speakers stay on
and look within for sustenance.

> *I was a leader among my friends. . . .*
> *We still see each other socially.*
> *We have what we call a Social Friends Club.*
> *We meet once a month in each others' homes.*

> *If things would only stay the same,*
> *we would be content.*

Turning inward, they stay on, hold on to old values,
old ways, and to jobs with clouded futures.
They know they ought to make a change.

> *I'm fifty-seven. I've been in this mill twenty-five*
> *years, and I'm still a loom mechanic.*
> *They passed me over for foreman five years ago.*
> *I should have left then. I feel I could*
> *do something better—make a change.*

Lost and sad at missed opportunities, still these
fiercely independent people share a common voice—
the voice of working America in a time that's gone forever.

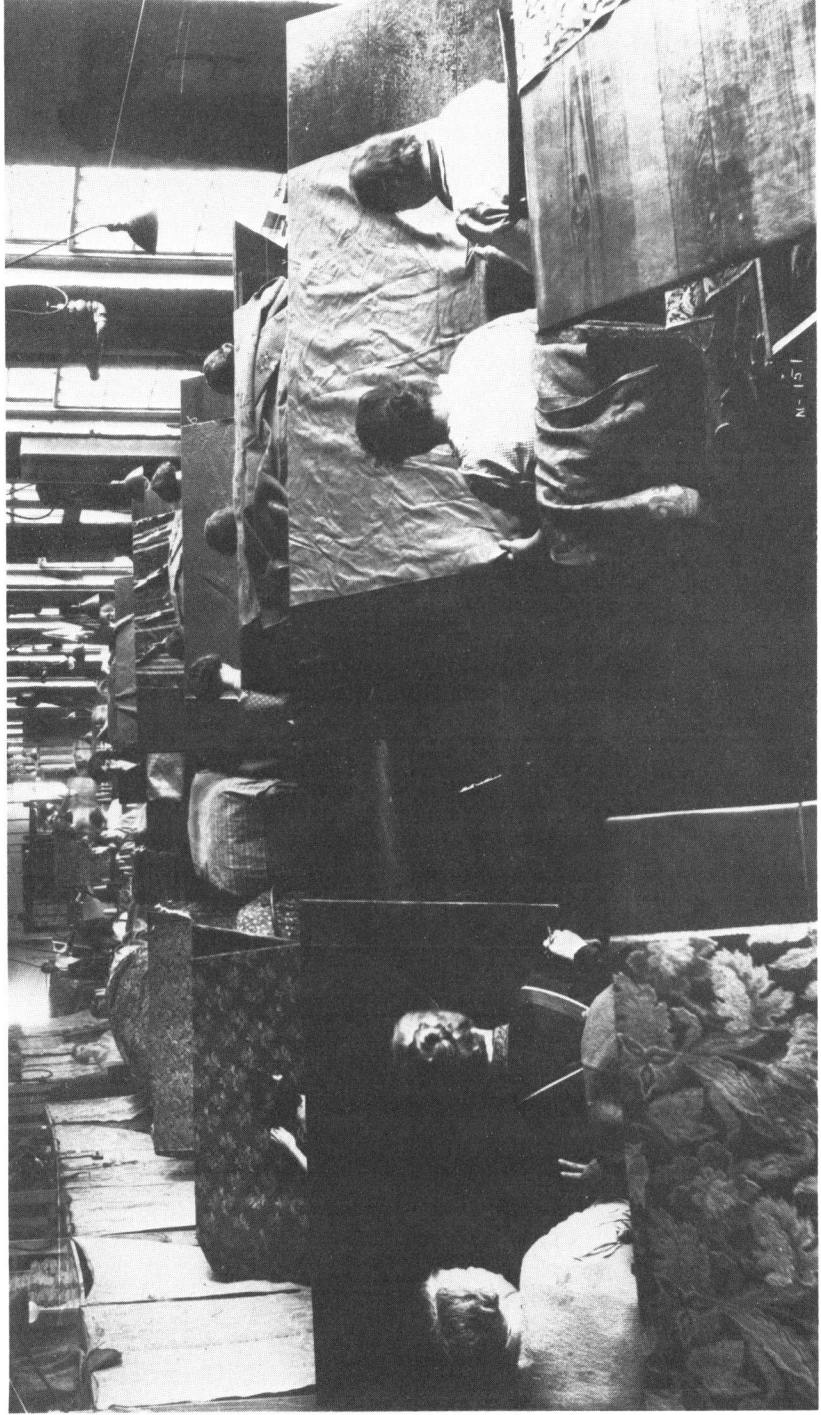

Jean Seder
Author and Fellow Worker

Father came to Philadelphia in 1910 to work for the Pioneer Suspender and Belt Company. Recognizing his potential, the company gave him considerable responsibility, including his own secretary.
She was tall and slim, with blue eyes and black hair. A country girl from Carbondale, Pennsylvania.
"I admired him so," she told me.
"He was so hard-working, so ambitious. He was Jewish, and I had never met a Jew before, but from the first, I loved him."

In his room at night father invented a belt buckle with interchangeable initials. Instead of engraving, the right combination of loose metal letters could be snapped into the buckle.
The reply from the Patent Office was intercepted by the president of the company who demanded the rights for the company. The end result was a contract to buy my father's invention, and he left to start his own business.

His secretary went with him.
"When I read that contract, and saw what he had done, where he was going, I wanted to go with him," she told me.
They were married on their lunch hour and returned to work to finish out the rest of the day.

Father bought a run-down mill in Kensington, and set out to make upholstery fabrics.
He knew nothing about textiles, but he hired a plant manager who did.
Mother took her place as his secretary, bookkeeper, clerk, personnel manager, purchasing agent, chauffeur, and moral support.
As soon as we were able, my brother and I helped out. We settled down after adolescence into a routine of work in a family business that we have never left.
At first I helped with the filing. I learned the switchboard.
My brother worked on the yarn crew, supervised inventories, and during summers took over as watchman. As he got older he went on selling trips with father.
On my brother's graduation from college, father arrived with a new car for him. In the back seat, neatly piled, was our new line of samples. My brother had a yearning to go to law school, but a salesman was needed to cover the Chicago area.
He took the wheel. Since then he has built a sales force that covers most of the country, and now he is president of the company.
Many people replaced my mother.
The billing is computerized. We have secretaries, a ticket office, a purchasing agent, a designing force, plant foremen, and various clerks to handle the myriad paper work.
I gave my father the greatest gift of all. I married a young lawyer and brought him into the business.
He re-organized our cost system, brought order to our dealings with the government, the union, our suppliers, and slowly replaced my father.
Today he is chairman of the board of one of the last successful textile mills in Kensington.

As for myself, I have worked at my husband's side doing the thing I do best—keeping contact with the workers.
I have known them—the old-timers—all my life. I grew up with them: the menders, bobbin-pullers, sweepers, and yarn men.
I have worked with the tall, gaunt colored men who lift the heavy yarn boxes every day to store them neatly, repack the broken ones, and keep their records straight. I have worked with the winders to put

away their stock in ordered places, and to use it. I've kept after an endless succession of young men who feed the bobbins into the looms to stay at their stations, do their jobs right.

I have gone to Christmas parties, picnics, weddings, and funerals; and while today the young people come and go, the old-timers and I have forged a bond of understanding and friendship which, when we are gone, will never be replaced.

At this time in our lives, however, in this area, we are all winding down.

Almost all the other mills have gone. The textile giants of the South—non-unionized, computerized—have undersold and out-produced the northern mills.

We survive because our designs and quality lead the field.

At the time my husband came into the business, he hired a young German refugee named Henry Schott. He was put in charge of designing.

Completely self-assured, Henry proceeded to take over the purchase of yarns and the production of fabrics in the mill. He designed, bought the yarn, adapted design to loom, and supervised the weaving of it.

Before long he had the foremen reporting to him, and he was hiring and firing.

He met every challenge head on.

He knew how to fix a loom. He knew how to weave as well as the weavers. He won their grudging respect.

He worked at a pace that left no time for diplomacy.

He worried my father who felt his plans extravagant and ambitious, and he annoyed my brother by refusing certain orders. In fact, Henry outraged everybody except my husband who recognized his genius and quietly supported him.

As years went by, Henry's fabrics not only sold, they became famous in the field. No one could match him for innovation, bold color, clever inventiveness.

Henry's designing genius plus the driving force of our family have kept the business going in spite of recessions, competition, and rising costs.

But today we are all in our sixties.

None of our sons is interested in coming into the business.

Our building is surrounded by shells of old factories.

Our watchmen wage an endless battle with the children of the neighborhood who harass them and vandalize the building.

Rolls of tapestry are stolen.

The neighbors surrounding us now seem hostile.
They refuse to be responsible for their children.

The era of working together—paternal employer, old and loyal employee—is gone.
My husband still gives our workers legal advice and lends them money at no interest. They used to come to him with family problems and he would mediate. He wrote their wills. He "knew" someone at City Hall. He went to court with them when a child got into trouble. Only the old-timers come to him now with their personal problems.

The old friends that I know grieve with me over the changes we see within the mill and in their neighborhoods.
They are not sentimental. They see what's happening.
Yet, like myself, they keep on working each day, staying where they are, unable (or is it that we are unwilling?) to make a change.

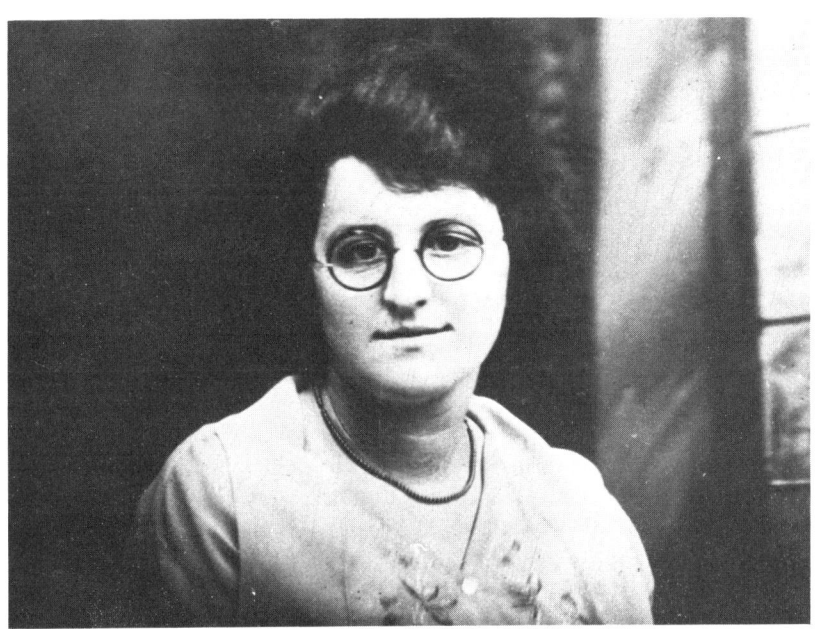

Mother and Son: Irene Brown

Early Kensington Resident

I'm eighty-eight now, but I remember very clearly.
I was born in Fishtown, across from Palmer Park in one of those little Revolutionary Father-Son-Holy Ghost houses.
1348 East Palmer, just down from Saint Mary's where I was christened. Each floor held only one or two rooms.

We called it Fishtown because they smoked fish. There were many smoke houses.
You bought your fish right there, in a brown paper bag. At home you'd heat it, right in the bag. Oh! It was delicious!
Maybe we called it Fishtown because many boat captains lived there. Many famous tugboat captains. Ernest Plumer. Peter Martin. He had the biggest tug on the river! He lived on Berks Street, between Belgrade and Thompson. It's called Kensington now.

It was colorful in those days. A lot went on. I remember an old lady used to come down our street on weekends, selling her home-made soup. She'd sing out:
"Peppery-Pot! Peppery-Pot!
Nice and Hot! Nice and Hot!"
It would be eleven o'clock, sometimes midnight when she'd come by. Why so late, I don't know, unless she figured people would be hungry by that time. They would go out and buy. Twenty cents a bowl it was. She made it herself.
On weekend nights this man would come through singing with this megaphone. He'd sing "Marta," "Rambling Rose," . . . Sundays he'd sing "The Old Rugged Cross." People threw him money.
He was lame.
The men got together then too. There were quoit games running continuously on the weekends, on a lot between Jasper and Emerald. If a man felt like a game of quoits on a Saturday night, he could just stroll out and take his turn.

My parents ran a small grocery store, and spelled each other working long hours. My father kept the store open evenings. I remember watching him coming back late at night up Belgrade Street. It wasn't paved yet, and his shoes would be caked with mud. He would come into the house so weary.
There were five of us. We were cultured. Refined. Sister Alma played the piano. I played the violin. We were encouraged to bring our young men home. Mother never objected as long as she could see us. Two of my sisters never married. They could have. They seemed to just want to work and come home to take care of mother.
A lot of good Catholic girls do that.

I was the first to marry. I had six children. Tom, my oldest, went to work in a textile mill at fourteen. He started out sweeping and now he's the Shipping Foreman. He and his wife bought a taproom last year. It's called The Brown Jug. They are making out very well. Saturday nights he has a singing group around his player-piano.
A real following.
Joe went into the service. Mike is a barber. Has his own shop.
The girls all went to business school and work as stenographers in big offices.

After my husband died and I was alone with the children still young, I remember how good my neighbors were. Many the night Mrs. McGuinnis next door would come over with a hot platter. Once when

I was sick, she came in every morning to cook and get the children off to school for me. So good she was.

I live with my daughter Mary now. We had a family picnic last summer. One hundred and ten came! I have thirty-four grandchildren, eighteen great-grandchildren. If you write about me, that's the meaning of my life.

Tom Brown
Plant Manager

My parents were Irish all the way.
My father's parents were born in County Cork, Ireland.
They came here to make their fortune like everyone else.
Mother's folks were born here though. Irish descent.
Her grandfather's father fought in the Civil War.
Their name was Kennedy.

I was born in 1929 in Saint Mary's Hospital. That's in Holy Name Parish, which is really Fishtown.
When I was two years old we moved to the Harrowgate section of Kensington. And I have been here ever since.

My father had one arm. He lost it playing with firing caps on the railroad tracks. They were blowing up old tin cans. One of the cans cut him on the arm. He got blood-poisoning. In those days they couldn't do anything. They cut off his arm. He was eleven.

He and mother ran a very successful delicatessen-type grocery store.
Mother cooked and father sold the cookings—along with other things.
Mother was a very good cook, and they made a prosperous living
from the store until the depression hit. They lost the store in 1931.

People who dealt in those kind of stores dealt on the book, you know,
and they began not being able to pay. There were all these unpaid
grocery bills. They lost everything, the business, their home—
everything!

So we rented a home on Emerald Street.
There were six of us children then.
Father spent the depression out of work. Naturally. People with two
arms couldn't get jobs. Who's going to hire a man with one arm?
He sold soap from door to door.
We helped.
As soon as I was able I carried groceries home for people. Ran
errands. John worked in an airplane factory. The girls got secretarial jobs.
We lived happily, but we were very, very poor. I remember
sitting with no electricity. Mushroom soup was a good meal.
Mother, though, could take kidneys—anything—and make a good meal.
She could take ground meat and make it taste like turkey!
She was a very good cook.

So we lived as best we could. I remember the bad things and I
remember the good things, like sitting around the radio listening to
our favorite programs together. We could sit and entertain ourselves
in the parlor, singing songs, singing old songs. Things like that.
We didn't even have a piano. We just used to sing together.
My mother was a great singer.

I was a leader among my friends. We used to play games in the streets
all summer long. I remember those long summer evenings.
I was usually the captain.
We'd draw up sides and play "Steal the Bacon" or "Ring-A-Leevio."
"Steal the Bacon" was a matter of two teams lining up about ten feet
from the "bacon," which could be anything—a hat, a book.
The person in the middle called a number, like, say, two. If that was
your number, you had to run in and grab the "bacon" before
anybody from the other team caught you.
"Ring-A-Leevio" was our favorite. You chose sides and set off a place
for a prison. One team had to catch all the ones from the other team

and put them "in prison." But if you were still free, you could run out and through the prison shouting "Ring-A-Leevio!" That would set all your teammates free. We loved that game.

Many of my friends are married now, but they still live in the neighborhood. We still see each other socially. We have what we call a Social Friends Club. We meet once a month in each others' homes. And we do different things together, too. Occasionally, we go away on weekends—maybe only to Cherry Hill Inn in New Jersey. We have dinner and stay over Saturday night.

We were all married twenty-five years in 1976, and we all went on a cruise together. We went on the S.S. Rotterdam to Nassau.

This summer we're planning to go to Vermont.

I went to Saint Joan of Arc for eight years and then to North Catholic High School. But I dropped out in my junior year and went to work in a textile mill. I don't know. I didn't like school. High school didn't really mean that much to us in those days.

When the job opportunity came up, I just took it. My parents minded. There was much argument, and

"You'll be sorry! You'll be sorry!"

I never have been.

I started out as a yarn receiver in the cellar. We took in big cartons of yarn, sometimes over three hundred pounds. It was hard work but I didn't mind. I was strong as an ox as a kid. We used to work very hard and get our work done, and then we'd set up a little tennis court in the basement and play in our spare time. We took our breaks when we wanted to. We'd work like hell for whatever time it took to catch up, and then we'd have a little fun. I remember in the fifties we had a bowling team, and I also formed a softball team and managed it.

In 1960 the company bought a second building and they put me in charge of it. I was in charge of everything—the shipping, the mending, the yarn crew. *Everything.*

I think I've done a good job. I'm a take-charge guy.

I have five children. Three of my boys are working here in this building under me. My girls are married and are housewives. Never had any serious problems with them. I am a strong father. I am well respected because I demand it. I think that's where it is. It's in the home. We were always a close family.

I remember during World War II when we were living in the house on Emerald Street. Two of my sisters were married, but when their husbands went off into the Service, they came home to live with the family. We squeezed them in. They were working, you understand, but they came home to live with us for the duration.

I never think about retirement. I did try running a taproom on the side, but it was too much for me. I couldn't do both. While I had it I was famous for my Saturday night sing-a-longs. People came from all over the city to sing with us. I'm an Irish tenor. I'll sing at the drop of a hat.

I guess you'd say I'm in a rut, but I've been satisfied here. The only thing I feel I might of done different was go into politics. I'm in politics now, in a small way, in my neighborhood. I've got a friend who intends to run for Mayor in the next election. I'm helping him. If he wins, then I'll really get involved. You might say that's my hobby. I'm good at it.

Gus Misuinas

Hosiery Spinner

I was born in Vilna, Lithuania, in 1893. It's Russia now.
I can remember in my mind the church I was christened in. We were Roman Catholic.
I went to school, but only for one year. Mother took me out to help at home. Father was away in the army.
When he came home, conditions were so bad he decided we should go to America. He had a friend who had gone. Word came back one could get a good job with the railroads. It turned out his friend was a porter in a railway station in Philadelphia.
Father got a job working in a nail factory. It must have been enough to bring us over because we came. I was eleven. I went to school here one year, but I couldn't understand the English.
I couldn't understand anything!
When I was twelve, mother went to City Hall and got my working papers. That was 1906.

I went to work at Second and Allegheny Streets at the Tommy Brown Hosiery Factory. We made cotton stockings. I was a helper on a

machine. I got $2.50 a week. I worked from seven to six P.M., and on Saturdays from seven to two P.M. I didn't like it.
The hours were too long.
I quit three or four times thinking I could find something else—something better for me. Never had no luck. Nobody wanted kids. I'd take my lunch and act like I was going to work, so Mother wouldn't know I'd quit. But she found out when I couldn't turn over my pay. I had to go back.
After a while I got so I didn't mind. I learned to be a knitter. They paid you piece work. Four and a half cents a dozen stockings. I could make forty dollars a week if I didn't have a breakdown.

I met my wife in 1913, at a christening. She was half German, half Polish. We had two kids, a girl and a boy.
My girl married Walter Adamczyk, who owns this tavern where I live now. She died of diabetes ten years ago, and Walter married again. But he lets me live on here. I don't get on with his new wife. She'd like to throw me out.
I don't see my boy anymore, so I can't go there. I never felt welcome in his house when I visited.

I used to bicycle and walk a lot.
I loved to walk! I used to go out walking on Sundays for miles. Sometimes I took the boy and made him walk too. Coming back we'd ride the trolley.
I used to ride my bike too. One time I rode out as far as Norristown! I got a flat and had to push the damned thing back. I stopped and asked a cop how far it was to Second and Tioga.
"My God!" he says. "That's thirty miles!"

Trains, autos and bikes was my hobby.
The daughter got me started on model trains. I spent a lot of money on them. But when she died, I lost interest.
Sold them dirt cheap to a guy who came in the bar one day. Sold my tools too. Now I don't do nothing but sit around.

I remember one time, before my old lady died, I had a stroke and was in the hospital. They said I was dying, but I was fighting like hell to live.
"What are you fighting for?" the wife says. "What have you got to live for?"
Well, to tell you the truth, I was just fighting for my life. Our girl had died, and I didn't have a job anymore. The company had shut down, but I wanted my life.

The problem is there's not much I feel like doing. Mostly I just sit around here now.

Last year I got this dog. I named him Mugsy. He was good company. Used to sleep with me. He'd sit at the bar and entertain the customers. Sit up and beg for pretzels.

But you know how it is with a dog in a bar. I'd get to drinking and forget to take him out. He'd go in a corner and pee. Walter's old lady would get mad.

One day she got so mad, she offered Mugsy to one of the customers in the bar.

"Sure," he says. "I'll be over for him Tuesday."

That was that. It was her place.

I guess she'd like to get me out of here.

Give me away too!

Well, if I could think of some place to go—I would.

Catherine Hutt
Mother

Father built our house himself, on Thompson and Wheatsheaf Lanes in Richmond. 1890.
He came over from Germany. Mother was Dutch. Father owned sixteen lots and the big farmhouse. We had horses, chickens and twelve cows! We had a good life.
My father worked during the day in a rope works factory while us kids and mother took care of the animals. Mother sold the milk. I used to help her. We'd go out on the wagon every morning. People would come out with their containers and we'd dip it out.
Milk was only four cents a pint then. The poor people used to come and ask for two cents worth. When they did that, Mother would fill their cups for nothing. I would be rich today if I could collect from all the people that owed us. When it was time to collect the milk bill, they would see us coming and hide. Or, they would give me what they had. I used to come home from collecting with pies, cakes, vegetables . . . Mother was too good hearted. But we were happy. We wanted for nothing.

When I was twelve years old, I went to work in the Wolstenholm Knitting Mills. I ran a spool box. I worked from 6:30 in the morning until six at night. I wore long skirts as if I was a grown woman. I got four dollars a week.

I gave my salary to Mother because everything had gone by then. They sold the animals. It wasn't as good as when we had them.

Well, I had worked two years at Wolstenholm when they fired me. I'll tell you why.

I was big and full of fun. I was a leader among the girls. I used to get the girls together and I'd say, "Let's strike!"

Not that I had any particular reason. I wanted to see some fun. It was boring, you know. We just wanted to see some excitement.

Then, sometimes, just to get a "bum," I'd make bad work and blame the machine. They'd send someone to fix the machine and I'd have a "bum."

After that I settled down, though. I got a job at a paper mill called Herbs. All I did was fold the ends of each roll as they came out.

I hated it, but I stayed until I got married.

I married a boy from our group. He was German, and we lived in the same neighborhood.

In those days, neighbors were friendly. In the summer the men played cards in the street. People sat on their porch steps and everybody spoke to you.

Juniata was all park then. There were springs with clear, cold water. Everybody would go up to the park. All the kids. We'd pick apples and pears and sit right down there and eat them!

Friday was clean-up day. Everybody washed down their front steps and swept the sidewalks. The streets too. Everybody would work together. Help each other.

The boys used to go swimming in the Delaware River. Most of the time they'd swim naked. If the cops came, they just wouldn't get out of the water!

You could get a boat at Allegheny and Delaware Avenues and go down the river to "Soupy Island." We called it that because you got a free bowl of soup on the way.

My husband bought a pack of books and taught himself to be an electrician. He got a job at American Engineer Company as an electrician's helper. He used to go out on Sundays and wire houses for extra money.

He could fix anything!

I didn't go out to work any more. We had six kids.

But I spent it faster than I made it.
I was young, you know. Wound up with nothing on Sunday.

Kensington Avenue used to be nice. It had a lot of movie houses back then. There was a boxing area, too. It was called The Non-Pareil. But its nickname was "The Blood-Pit." A ticket cost twenty-five cents. We had good fighters. See-Saw Kelly, Philadelphia Jack O'Brian. Johnny Jadick. Eddie Cool. Them two names went into the Boxer's Hall of Fame!

From the boxing area, for the next six blocks, it was all stores and movie houses. It was called Band-Box Row. It's not so nice today. What we used to do was walk down the avenue at night and get a plate of ice cream. Today you pay thirty-five cents for a little cone. In those days you could get a big dish for fifteen cents. There was this one place famous for its ice cream. "Cooks," on Kensington Avenue. They moved away, though.

Another thing we did a lot was have block parties. Different social clubs would give them. Eight or ten fellows could form a club. I belonged to a club called "The Somersets." I was the secretary.
At the block party we'd dance to a five or seven piece band.
The bands got five or ten dollars.
Lots of food for sale, too. That's where my money went!

Lots of times we'd take a boat ride down the river.
The "Wilson Q" went to Riverview Beach, down Wilmington way. If we went up, we went to Burlington Island, across from Bristol. There was an amusement park there. You got to it by ferry.
It got burned down in 1927.
My sister had a little shack on the island. A summer place. People still do. Nice places. My sister had her own boat. When we'd go for a visit, this man would row us over for five cents.

Well, I got tired of changing jobs.
My God! I couldn't tell you what all I didn't do!
I worked for a while in a wet wash. We pulled the wash out of the tubs and wrung it through the wringer.
When you're young you don't mind changing jobs. But I got to longing for a real profession.
So I decided to become a textile card cutter.
I asked for a job at a card cutting firm at Clearfield Avenue. "Walter W. Hodgson's," it was called. Now it's controlled by the Neveling

boys. Anyway, they would only let me drive the truck because to cut cards you had to join the Card Cutters' Union.
After that, it took ten years to learn.
"If you get a job here, we'll teach you," the shop steward said.
"If the Union will teach you, we'll give you a job," Mr. Hodgson said. So all I could do was drive the truck.
That's the way those union fellows was.

Well I finally got into that union, in 1946. They had only twenty men left out of fifty or sixty. They were all old. They kept retiring or passing away until there was only two left. They were so damned careful not to let any young men in, it ruined the union. Now we all belong to the Textile Workers.
You know, thousands of young people go to textile school now, but nobody comes out a card cutter. I don't know why.
Anyway, I had a friend cutting cards at another mill.
He let me hang around and watch. Fool with the machine.
So I taught myself.
But I still had to go into the union as an apprentice. I really got in because they needed someone to do a job, and there was no card cutter available. They knew I knew how, so they took me in.
I got forty dollars a week.

I worked at Hodgson's until 1955 and got to be a full-fledged union member. I made big money. One hundred fourteen dollars a week! But then things got slow and we went part-time. So when the Neveling Company called me, I went. But there we were on piece work. So much a card. Ten cents it was.
If you cut two hundred cards a day, you made twenty dollars.
Well, I didn't like piece work. You worked so hard to make enough. So when I saw an ad in the paper for a card cutter at Moss-Rose Company, I called. They paid union wages, and no piece work. What a relief!

I've been here ever since. Craftex Mills bought Moss-Rose out in 1960. Nobody said nothing to me, so I kept on working. A lot of people left, but I'm still here, card cutters being scarce, you know.
I'm seventy-two now. Ought to retire. But Craftex keeps sending over jobs for me to do. So, I just keep on working.
My only girl's a nun. Teaches school. I'm all alone at home.
I guess when they stop sending over cards, I'll stop. But I can't rightly think what I'll do then. This is my life, you know.

Joe Barker

Textile Weaver—Loom Fixer

I was only one year old when the flu came out. That was 1917.
We lived on American Street . . . same houses that blew up from a gas break last year. You probably read about it.
There was a terrible shortage back then in houses.
You were lucky to get a house!

My father was a loom fixer. Cloth. He used to work down at Reeves, in Kensington.
He used to go back and forth to the old country though. He went to England seven times! Why? Because he was a wanderer.
Mother was a weaver. She went back and forth to England a couple of times herself. Matter of fact, they knew each other over there. Just from seeing each other.
Used to be a popular sport at the pubs over there to throw each other out the door. Nothing vicious about it. Just friendly stuff.
There was this friend of my father's, Jack Benson. They came over to the states together. Matter of fact, Jack introduced my mother to my

father over here. But like I said, she already knew him from over there.

I used to go to the Adams School. It's torn down now.
Did I tell you about the kids who used to get out on the fire escapes and walk around the building on its girders? Scared the mothers. Same thing in the playground. We used to go down this big sliding board on our roller skates.
Everybody hollers about what kids do now-a-days. You shoulda seen some of the things we used to do. We played soccer, volley ball. Anything at all to kick the ball around. Made up the rules as we went along.
Then there was always somebody tryin' to terrorize ya. They made you learn to defend yourself. Wasn't nothin' vicious. They just beat you up friendly like. They used to take the scariest kid in school and chase him around.
There was this one kid named "Caesar." The time they had that Edward G. Robinson picture? Well, naturally, he was associated with it. He belonged to the Abigail Street Gang. That was a little street between Amber and Trenton Avenue.
Those kids were all Golden Glove fighters. They used to chase me around when I was only in the fourth grade.
I remember one day Caesar had me cornered. Well, I skeetered out somehow and jumped a six-foot fence. I went home and cried to my sister. She had been in the habit of doing my arguing for me. This time she got tired of defending me and told me if I didn't go back and beat him up—she'd beat me up! So I went back, and this time I won! I came back real proud.
Caesar never bothered me after that. Neither did nobody else. He put a protectorate on me. I only figured that out later. I used to go down to all these different neighborhoods and nobody bothered me. All those kids in the Abigail Gang—they knew me. I didn't know who they were, but they knew me!
That was the situation.

I never earned money when I was a kid.
I never was a hustler. My brother was.
He was always selling pretzels at the Swim-O. Flowers, shoe shinin'—you name it. Always makin' a buck somehow. Like I said, some kids are hustlers. Some ain't.

I used to go to school on roller skates. It was a mile and a quarter. When it got icy, the skates worked like ice skates.

I wasn't interested in school. All we did was copy out of books. Each class was the same way—copy page after page, be quiet—so I decided to leave in the eleventh grade.

My mechanical drawing teacher was distraught about it because he figured on making me a draftsman. I could read straight off the prints and ink right off a draft. I think he had a job lined up for me, but I didn't know about that until I left.

Well, my father said either go to school or go to work. So I went to work with my father. The company paid me five dollars, and dad paid me five. What I did at first was waltz the broom around. Then this woman, Emma Newson, taught me to weave.

In those days you either paid to learn, or you just stood there and watched 'til you learned.

I stood with Emma.

On the first day the noise of the looms made me numb. They woke me up at twelve o'clock—I was standing there asleep from the buzz of the looms. It's the same thing in this place. I watch the new help goin' 'round, and I always tell them, "After a while, you won't mind it."

When things got slow, in 1930, my dad was laid off. So was I. But I got a job right away at Twitchells. We made piano scarves. Dad never did work again.

We lived in a nice neighborhood without commotion where kids were under control. Parents had control of the situation then. Today! Kids run the streets at three o'clock in the morning! Six-year-old kids run around half-gassed.

Can't figure what happened. According to the trends today, it's the same all over. No matter where you go. Same pattern.

When I was young, we were more individual. We had good times. We used to go down to this ice cream parlor, Spars. It was high class. One side was ice cream and the other was a bar. If you wanted, you could have ice cream with your beer.

Movies were a big part of life, too. The movie houses were so nice! They had live stage shows with the movie, and they gave away dishes and glasses. We didn't care if it was hail, sleet or snow; my wife and I went to the movies Tuesday nights to get our dish.

Ever hear about the Battle of Waterloo? This particular block, Waterloo Street, (it's a playground now) had all those Father-Son-Holy Ghost houses. They had three rooms straight up, a toilet out in the back yard, and heat from the kitchen stove. These houses weren't owned, you know; they were rented. It was a good investment.

They were sure of getting their rent in those days. You paid your rent first. The next thing you bought was food. After that, you got your coal. That's the way it worked.

Well a lot of Irish people lived on Waterloo Street. They used to get along pretty well during the week. But on weekends, when they got a little drunk, they used to have a battle. They'd get out in the middle of the street and have a fist fight. Nobody got murdered, and from what I could figure, nobody got seriously hurt. It was more like a friendly fight.

They had a special detail of police with this paddy wagon assigned to York Street. They were Irish cops that knew the people well. They'd go out and scoop 'em up and throw 'em in the wagon and take 'em down to the station for the night. They were out next morning.

You know, they'd be fighting in the middle of the street and, if a woman would come along on her way to the avenue, they'd stop fighting and let her pass. They they'd start up again.

I used to go back and forth there myself when I was courting my wife. Nobody bothered ya if they didn't know ya. But, if you were looking for an argument, you could get one fast enough. That went on for years.

I came to this place to work in 1949—been a loom fixer here ever since.

What I do with my spare time is read. I do a lot of reading, but I don't keep books. I pass them on when I'm finished.

I could've gone to college, but I didn't have a retentive memory. Everybody's born with certain qualifications. I was interested in radio when I was a kid. I could build a transmitter, but I never got the amateur license because I couldn't remember the code. What I'm trying to get at is, I could build the thing, but I couldn't pick up the letters and put them together in my head. Yet some people have told me I'm brilliant.

I invent things. I invented a coil to save energy in batteries and to make sparkplugs last forever. But I never applied for a patent. Use it in my own car, though. It has a hundred thousand miles on it so far and is still going strong.

Thinking on this college thing. You know, some guys go through college because they have remarkable retention, but they ain't got the brains of a roach.

When I retire I really don't know what I'll do. I've got no plans—never make plans. They don't work out. The best laid plans of mice and men—

We were taught you never get nothin' for nothin'. Right? I read the papers from end to end, but there's nothin' in them no more. They're getting less and less interesting.

Listen, there's nothin' much to write about me. My sister was interesting. She was a weaver, too, but she's mad now because they retired her. You know, a lot of people don't like that—being retired.

Duo:
Marion Knuttel

Textile Winder

I was born at home. Palethorpe Street in Kensington.
My parents were German.
In my childhood, kids played games in the street. We just had fun together. "Jump rope." "Hopscotch." "Baby-in-the-air." "Dodge ball."
"Tin can." "Hide-go-seek."
We didn't have much. I knew better than to ask for anything. But we had good times. My parents took us to the big parks—Woodside, Willow Grove—but we never went on rides. We just walked around. You learn. They don't have it. You don't ask.

Sometimes we'd visit relatives in Logan. A lot of German people lived in Logan. We went by trolley for seven cents. Little kids rode free on Sundays. Once we went to Baltimore on the bus!

We used to listen to the radio a lot together. The Shadow. Jack Armstrong. Little Orphan Annie. Secret Message.

There was a steel mill at the end of our street. The men who worked in there would let us kids in the yard to play. It was a beautiful grass lawn and the men made a swing for us on a tree. We girls would take our dolls and our doll coaches in there, and we'd play. We'd never touch or hurt nothing. Everybody played together there.
Sometimes we'd go down to Diamond Street Square Park. We'd get all the kids on the block (I was twelve) and we'd have a picnic. We'd have a good time all day long. Played games. Got along. We weren't scared of anything. We didn't have nobody to be scared of in those days. Seems like the kids were happier years ago.

I had to do housework, you know. If I didn't do it right, I did it over. We had linoleum on all our floors. I had to scrub those floors twice a week.
And you didn't sass your mom because if you did, she'd hit you.

I wanted to be a dressmaker, only I went to the wrong school. I went to Kensington High School. I should have went to trade school. Anyhow, I quit at sixteen and got a job at a place that made surgical belts and trusses. I was a paster. I learned to operate a sewing machine there. It was eighteen dollars a week.
No union. We worked from eight to five—half hour for lunch. They didn't push us, though. You done your job. That was all.
I stayed two years. Then I went to a place called Twitchells. They made auto seats. I was a mender, or burler.
I learned to wind there. We had old-fashioned frames. You had to pull the handle each time you put the bobbin in. It was tiring, but I got good money. Fifty dollars a week!

I got married at nineteen.
My husband was the foreman of the winding room. He was Polish.
I had five kids. Two miscarriages. Seems like they were all little at one time.
We bought a little bungalow in the Wissinoming section for six thousand dollars. Four rooms and a bathroom. Two bedrooms.
And I ended up with five kids in there! I hung 'em from the ceiling!

My last kid was John. When he was born I didn't know what was the matter. I thought he was just fat and lazy. When he was eight months, I took him to St. Christopher's. They called me in and told me he was retarded and fifty percent blind.

Well, I took him home and done the best I could for him. I loved him and tried to learn him things. I got him into a little school run by Lutheran sisters, and he was happy there.

My daughter Jane was the one who was especially good to him. She never hit him, and she took care of him if I was working and he was home. They were all good to him but she done the most.

When he was nine, I got him into a good school at Rivercrest, but they told me he could only stay until he was thirteen. I was worried about when he'd be a man, you know. Who would take care of him then?

Through a friend, I got him into Pennhurst, where he can stay for the rest of his life. We go up and see him every other weekend and bring him home for the holidays.

He's six feet tall now. Nobody can handle him any more when he's home, but me.

My husband always was a heavy drinker, but at some point he started drinking too heavy. He'd come all hours from the bar and start a fight. Always fighting and cursing. I had him before a judge four or five times.

That's why I think my oldest boy is so nervous today. He has his father's disposition. He don't want to, but he does.

I tried to stay home with John, but we needed money. So I took a job at Craftex Mills as a winder.

I met a weaver there named Joe Knuttel. He gave me the strength to leave my husband.

I married Joe.

People tell me I have a happy disposition. Things don't go right, I don't let it worry me too much.

You learn to accept things. You can't sit and brood. If I did, I'd be sitting in a corner, crying.

When my youngest daughter Jane told me she was pregnant, I was terribly upset. She was only sixteen and he was seventeen. But then I calmed myself.

I told them not to get married. To wait. So they agreed.

Jane had the baby and I took it in. Jane finished school.

Now Jane works on the first shift and I take care of the baby. Then I work on the second shift and she takes over. So, we're raising him together.

Seems like now I still have children all over the place! My kids bring their kids home so they can go off.
Well, I don't mind. I love them all.
It would be nice if Joe and I had a bigger place and more time to ourselves; but listen, we have good times.

Joe Knuttel

Textile Weaver—Loom Fixer

Mother came from Hungary. Father from Germany.
I was born in Kensington Hospital, 1931.
Father was a baker. When he first came to this country he worked in a bar. He liked to have a good time and all, but he saved his money.
He didn't get married 'til late, so when he met my mother he was able to buy a bakery store. He had his bake ovens in the garage next to our house.
He learned to bake in the army over in Europe. He said he never carried a gun, just a roasting pan. He made a point of that with us kids.
"Never carry a gun. No need for it."
If we got into trouble, we had to figure it out.
If we lost a fight, we never said anything.
Father was good natured, and a good man. A good provider.

We grew up in the house on Hancock and Cambria. My sister runs the store there still. It's been over fifty years I guess.

I went to Saint Bonaventure. Most of the kids in our neighborhood went to "Viso." That's Visitation School.
But we were German. Ours was strictly a German parish. So we went to Bonaventure.
The Irish kids went to "Viso."

When I was in high school, my father got very sick and we started to run out of money. It turned out he had leukemia, but we didn't realize it at first.
From the time I hit sixteen, he was going downhill fast.
I figured I'd better go to work. So I quit school. I had no great ambitions anyway.
I was interested in mechanics and that's what I am today.
A mechanic. I have no regrets.

I was thirty-seven when I married. I didn't want to get married earlier. I was enjoying running around.
When I first started working, I saved my money . . . like my father.
But then I got to thinking, "what for?" I says, "To heck with it!"
So I started going up to the mountains. Treating at bars. Getting drunk, sometimes every night.
After work, a gang of us would go to the clubs or have parties.
Raise hell.
Then the company offered me the job of straw boss on the third shift.
It seemed like when I went on the third shift, everything changed.
Guys got married. Teams started to break up. Like, the crowd just drifted apart.
I'll tell you the truth: I myself started to change. Slow down. It was like I dried up on the third shift. I used to come to work with a shirt and tie and go out with the guys afterwards. But when I was on the third shift, I'd get done and just go down to the Gin Mill and, after that, go home to bed. That was just about it on the third shift.
But then I met Marion Heise. She was on the second shift at the time. I got to coming early so we could talk. We began meeting weekends. Marion had five children and there were lots of problems, but I didn't care. I still had a little money saved. I wanted to get married.
I've never regretted it.

When I was a kid, before my father started getting sick, I'll tell you we had good times!
On Sundays, Father would take us on picnics. Down Sea Side.
Mom would fry porkchops and stuff the night before.

We were the lucky ones. We had a car! We were the only ones on our street who had a telephone, too!
Father used to make wine. We didn't have no backyard, but we had gardens in tubs on our roof.
Mom grew morning glories, chives, parsley, and things like that in big tubs on the roof. We were happy. Content.

I remember one day the people in back of us were pulling out the grass that grew between the cracks in their pavement. They thought they'd do us a favor and pull ours out too.
Mom came out and said, "What are you doing!"
They said, "Pulling out the grass."
Mom said, "The only thing green you have here in the city, and you want to pull it out?" She had a fit!

I had pigeons on our roof, too.
A guy at Rose Hill and Cambria sold them. A quarter a pair.
I'd take them out on the El to 69th Street and let them go.
They'd come home.
When I started having too many, my dad drove them and me out to a cousin's place in Tamaqua. Well, he kept 'em in a coop outside and a fox got 'em.
All except one which got away, and damn if he didn't make it home to me. Took him two weeks, but he came home.

Next to good times at home, I remember the games we used to play out in the street.
The most fun was "Buck-buck." Everybody lines up. You put your shoulder against the rump of the guy in front of you. The first guy leans against a lamp post or something. Then the other guys line up, and one by one they run and jump on top of you. Try to break you down.
"Pigeon-milk?" Ever play that? You line up in two sides. Then you grab ahold of a guy and say, "Pigeon-milk!" and put him in a chalk circle. The only way he can get out is for a kid on his side to grab ahold of him and say, "Pigeon-milk!" But there was a guard around the circle to stop him. It was kind of a tag game. We liked "Box-ball" too. You draw a square on the street. The pitcher bounces the ball on the ground. You hit it and start running the square. As soon as the pitcher catches it he yells out, "First base."
See, you don't need a big field that way. You can play on the street.
Then, of course, if everybody was busy, and there was just yourself, you could always play handball off any wall.

I don't go to church anymore. Marion is Protestant, and I'm lazy.
I keep religion in my heart, though. If I ever need it, I can fall back on it.
My father was that way. Toward the end, he was very devout.

Right now I'm going back to one of my old hobbies. Model airplanes. Just farting around with it.
The house Marion and I bought has a backyard. I grow vegetables and flowers. My specialty is roses.
How my mom would have loved that.

Matt Pytel

Textile Weaver—Loom Fixer

My parents settled in Port Richmond in 1923. We lived eighteen years on Webb Street in Kensington. I was born there. I'm Polish Roman Catholic.
My father was a tanner at Swoboda's. It's gone today.
When plastics came in, they threw leather out. They tell me leather's back in fashion.

We boys used to have a good time.
We used to swim naked in the Delaware River, underneath the Black Bridge at Richmond Street.
The cops would chase us, but everybody swam there.
We used to swim across the river to Petty's Island. We could fish there. Used to catch big catfish.
I was always a happy-go-lucky kid.
In the thirties, we stole coal out of the coal cars to heat our house.
It was a running battle with the yard police.
We didn't have electricity. We were really poor. But I don't remember it bothering me.

The Mutual Independent Company, at Tioga and the river, used to make fertilizer and dog food out of dead horses. The horses were killed right there.
They used to cut off the hooves and throw them away. We'd fish them out of the barrels and pry off the shoes and play "horseshoes" with them. You could buy a live horse from them for five dollars.

I went to work at seventeen on the Reading Railroad. Quit school and lied about my age. I wanted to get going, you know?
I went into the service in 1943. I got two battle stars for the battle of Remagen Bridge. Then I came back and got married.
I married Veronica Zarenkiwicz. We found a little house in Bridesburg.
I went to work as a bartender in my brother's saloon, but I'll tell you, I had a conflict. I loved to play baseball. I used to play baseball every evening. It was my life. I thought if I worked real hard on it,
I could go professional. So I quit my job.
But you know how it is. I was married and I had to earn money.
I had to stop being a kid.

So I went to work after that for a chemical company as a bull gang maintenance man. But I quit that too. The sulfuric acid they made there burned little holes in all my clothes. I hated it.
I came to this textile mill after that as a maintenance man. Then I learned to weave, and then I learned to be a loom fixer. There's better money in that. So now I'm a loom fixer still.
I'd like to quit—do something else. The company passed me over when they were looking for a supervisor for the first shift. They gave it to John Hutt.
I'm only fifty-four. There's no future for me here—nothing to look forward to.
Our girl is getting good pay as a special education teacher.
She's on her own. Has her own place.
We intend to keep our boy with us at home—forever.
That's no burden, really.
I feel I ought to take a chance and make a change.
But I just don't seem to do it.

Irene (Rocky) Dougherty
Textile Winder—Loom Magazine Filler

I was born on Elkhart Street in Kensington, 1941.
We're part Lithuanian, part German.
From Elkhart Street we moved to Jasper Street, to D Street, to Helen Street. It seemed like dad and mom weren't ever exactly satisfied.
The house on Helen Street was my grandparents'. We loved it there. It was near Harrogate Park where we used to play. When I was little, there was always a block party being held in the park.
If a family was in big trouble, like with a medical problem, their church would organize a block party for them. Everybody would come. There would be hot dogs and sauerkraut. Beer. A band for dancing.
Sometimes the Harrogate String Band would come out and play.
It was wonderful to see them—hear them. We kids would sometimes run out and pull a plume from one of the costumes for a prize.
A lot of money was raised for the family that way.

My grandfather was a chef in a big restaurant. Grandmom was a waitress. So even in the depression they saw to it there was plenty of food on our table.

But daddy wasn't happy living like that. One day he was taking a picture of me on our couch when over the radio came news of war declared. He decided he would go down for his physical that same day!

As soon as my mom got home from work he gave her a call. He told her to pack his bags and bring them down. They were taking him that day!

Mom swore he enlisted to get away from it all. There were just my sister and me. I couldn't understand it.

They sent my dad to Florida because he could speak German, and that's where the German prisoners were. He put in three years.

When he came home, he went to work for the Brown Instrument Company. He was the shop steward for many years.

Mom kept on working while dad was in the service because the allotment, you know, wasn't sufficient. She sewed parachutes.

She done something, my father said a lot of fellows didn't come back.

I loved school. I got along quite well with the nuns.

I loved English, history and art. But in parochial school, you don't get much art.

I went to public high school because my father wanted it. He had a thing against Catholics. He turned Catholic to marry my mother only for the day of the marriage. That was it.

I'd done fairly well until the tenth grade. You know how it is? You start cutting classes, so you don't do your homework. You start meeting boys and going to dances and everything. You know?

It all piled up on me.

One time my friends and I cut classes. We went to the Art Museum, for God's sake. I really wanted to see it. Well, we were wearing our high school sweaters, and a guard called up the school and reported us.

Can you imagine that? What a big stink!

They called in Mom and we had a big meeting. They gave me six months to pull up my marks.

So I said, "No." It got my back up. I quit.

I got a job at the Accuracy Scientific Instrument Company.

I mean that sounds heavy, doesn't it? They made industrial thermometers. We girls placed the thermometers in brackets to be engraved. It was like piece work. You had to do so many to get a bonus.

I made a dollar an hour. I was seventeen.

I met my husband when I was sixteen. I should have said no. He went to North Catholic. We went steady. We got married when I was twenty-one.
He worked at Towe Dye Company, Westmoreland and Frankford Avenue, running dye kettles. He wasn't making that much, but he was putting in an awful lot of overtime. Maybe fifteen, sixteen hours a day.
I kept on working too until I got pregnant with Joey.
We lived in an apartment on Strinber Street, a block from his parents. Well, Towe Dye started to get real slow. Finally they closed up and moved south.
I suggested to my husband he take the test for police officers. So he went down and took it and flunked. I told him to take it again.
So he did. This time he passed.
But we weren't getting along. We had constant arguments.
He never seemed to want to stay home. He was always at the taprooms. He never should have gotten married, really.
I didn't feel like staying home myself, by myself, so—I up and moved in with mom and dad.
Joey was two years old.

My nerves were getting so bad from sitting in the house, trying to figure out what to do, that I went to work again.
I got a job at Craftex Mills as a winder. That's when my good times started.
After work us girls on the first shift would go to Callahan's Taproom at the corner. We'd sit for hours and talk. Most times we'd be the only ones there.
I'd drink gin and tonic. Freda would drink Ortliebs. Mary would drink rum and coke. Rose would drink a mixture of things.
We'd play the juke box constantly.
We'd be there sometimes when the second shift would be coming in for lunch! 8:30 to 9 p.m. It would be everybody that walked in—you would know.
Mom and dad lived in the northeast by that time, but I wouldn't socialize up there. I'd hop a bus and go down to Kensington, because that's where the good times were.
We girls used to like to go to certain bars Friday nights. There would be a dance band and a lot of fellas. But we always stayed together.
Why drag somebody along that's going to ruin the evening?
We would play shuffleboard or darts and dance if we felt like it.
Sometimes we'd decide to go to the all-night clubs. Our favorite was on Venango Street.

Daddy told me that during the war they used to hold *Bund* meetings there. When the war was over it became a social club again.
You had to have a card to get in. That is, the men did. Not us girls. We would just ring the bell. We'd be standing there and this guy would open the door and look us over, and he'd say, "How many?" We'd say, "Four of us." And he would let us in.
You'd go downstairs and there'd be a nice band playing.
Our last resort was this little club we knew about near the mill. When everything else was closed, we'd go there.
You wouldn't even know what it was. You'd ring the bell and this guy would look out the window, and if he didn't know you, most likely you wouldn't get in.
But if it was a bunch of girls like Mary and me and Freda—I'll be honest with you, we were known all over Kensington—we'd get in there.
It was just a bar with tables in the back; but if you wanted a fast one for the road after all the other bars were closed, you'd go there.
We'd stay there until three in the morning. If I felt I couldn't make it home on the bus, I'd call my sister Marion. She didn't mind coming for me. I'd have to be really under though. We would usually make it home together.
Freda had a drinking problem, and you couldn't count on her staying with you. I mean, we'd be sitting on three bar stools, right? Me, Freda and Mary. When, all of a sudden, there'd be one empty stool! I don't have to tell you any further where Freda would be . . . on the floor right behind us!
We'd leave her there. She'd be all right because Freda was well liked in Kensington. She had a lot of protection. Any man that would attempt anything with Freda might as well write out his last will and testament. Freda didn't like to be bothered, especially by men.

Well, one day after work I came out and there was my husband, waiting. He wanted me to come back to him.
He was the type of guy who could never take no for an answer. If I told him to stay away, he'd come round. If I told him to come round, he'd stay away.
He always used to say, "Rocky, when you and I are seventy, I will still be chasing you."
I'm Catholic, and while I don't believe God would punish me, I, well, we were just—separated. Anyway, I was missing him and our relationship, which I realize now was only sexual.
I wasn't using my head. I wasn't thinking of Joey. That's the only time him and I ever got together again. But I got pregnant from it.

So now I have Helen Marie. She's six months old.
I had to hire a lawyer to get my husband to support her. He's always late in his payments. Always fighting it off.
One time he wanted me to take his lousy car instead of the seven payments he was owing.
Once he swore to the judge the baby wasn't his! Helen Marie and I had to go get blood tests!
Since the baby came, I don't go out anymore. Mom's getting older and she says she can't take it anymore.
Joey is so happy with me home all the time now.

I daydream a lot. One time I wanted to be a doctor. Our family doctor used to give me books to read. I was very good in chemistry. I loved biology.
I was good at art, too. I should have gone to art school. I would have been good at it. Sometimes I think of going at night now. But it's futile. I'm thirty-four.
Not that I couldn't if I set my mind to it. Today a woman can do anything she wants to. But it's the idea. You have to really, *really* want to.
I say to myself, "Rocky, if you had to do this for a living, could you?" And then I say to myself: "No."
Then there's Helen Marie and Joey. It's too hard.

I have this steady job at Craftex.
I have A-1 credit which I'm proud of. I fought damn hard for that! Separated girls have a terrible time getting credit.
They make it tough on women. Seems like they don't like it if a woman really means to make it on her own.

Samuel Berg
Shoemaker

I was born, 1918, right here in Kensington.
My father, though, was born in Hungary. He was sixteen when he came here. 1905.
My mother came in 1911. She was fourteen.
They didn't know each other.
She came to a relative at Forty-first Street. It was an uncle. She paid off the passage that he loaned her by doing housework. She worked as a houseworker for a family named Grossman. Mr. Grossman owned the Kensington Carpet Company.

My Dad came to New Market Street and opened a store.
He opened at New Market Street because there were a lot of foreigners who couldn't speak English. He could speak quite a few languages—Polish, Hungarian, Czechoslovakian. He did a nice business, simply because he could speak their languages.
He had tables full of pants, shoes, shirts. He knew shoemaking from the old country, but he did this thinking he could make more money.

But he went into business with his brother-in-law.
My father was the real salesman. The hard worker.
The other one went to the movies.
So my father saw he was being cheated. So, they split up. My father went back to his old trade. He opened a shoe repair shop on Kensington Avenue.

He met my mother, well, in Jewish they call it a "Shatchun."
He arranged a party at my uncle's house and five girls were invited. My father came and he was very direct.
He looked at them all and he pointed to my mother and he said, "I'll take that one."
Just like that. Like you're buying a suit. I don't know how she felt about it. It wasn't up to her. This was the way it was going to be. That's the way it was in those days.
You see, one of the reasons my mother was sent to this country was she was getting older, and they lived in the Carpathian mountains. There were no eligible men for her.
You might think fourteen was young, but that was considered time to get married, and her parents wanted a better future for her, so they persuaded the uncle to send the money.
She came alone. Now that I think about it, it must have been hard for her to do that, but—in those days you were expected to do as you were told. That's what they told her she had to do.
So my father chose her, and they got married.
They had five children.

I was the oldest boy.
Thinking of my father now, I realize he was psychotic. He used to beat me fiercely.
I don't know why. Anything would set him off. If a customer complained, or there wasn't enough money that week. Anything.
One time he chased me up Kensington Avenue, beating me as we ran. I was only a little child. I couldn't outrun him.
A woman stopped him and said,
"I'm going to have you arrested!" If she said that, it must have been pretty bad.
There were terrible fights at home, too, between my parents. Terrible shouting. Saturday mornings were the worst. It was terrible.

I loved school. I wanted to go to school, but it was difficult for me to learn because all those years it was emotional interference with intellect. You try to learn, but there's emotional interference.

You can't get it.
I went to the Horn School, Jones Junior High and Northeast High School.
I loved my years at Northeast!
You know, in those days the teachers at Northeast were older men.
A lot of them were Jewish. They knew their subjects and they loved to teach. You could tell.
They wanted to help you, they wanted you to learn, and they gave us such a sense of pride in ourselves.
They were sympathetic and they had a personal interest in each one of us.
We had to wear coats and ties and we were proud to be students there.
I used to walk down the avenue in my good suit, my coat and tie, and I wanted everyone to know I went to Northeast High School!
But when I'd get home after school, my father would make fun of me.
He'd say, "You think you look so swell in those fancy clothes?
Take 'em off and get to work in the shop, fancy guy!"
He'd make me feel like two cents.
I hated to come home.

The real fight between us was, I think, the violin.
I loved the violin. Oh, I loved music! My greatest dream was to be a violinist.
I shined shoes, simonized cars, ran errands, did odd jobs for neighbors; and I was able to buy a violin for sixty dollars.
I was between ten and twelve, I think. To start off, I took lessons from a man who owned a delicatessen store down the street from us.
He was an excellent violinist and he taught me for seventy-five cents a week.
I was getting very good. In fact, I was getting along too well.
He told me, "I think you should go to school now." He sent me to the Philadelphia Conservatory of Music.
I was doing well there, too, although it was much more difficult.
When you were told to do something, you were expected to know it by the next week!
But I was doing well—except for at home. My father didn't like it.
He kept saying I wasn't helping him enough in the store.
When I'd try to practice, he would say, "You will help me in the store!" And he didn't have enough work even for himself.
He domineered me. I was afraid of him. I think, had I not been afraid of him, I might have been a violinist today. That is what I wanted, what I'd still like to have.
When I hear a violinist play in a fine orchestra today, I know what he is doing. I think, that could be me.

I was twenty-three when the war came along.
Besides getting shrapnel in the front of my head, I lost a finger. So that settled the violin once and for all.
I was an anti-aircraft gunner in Newfoundland at first. I thought I'd be in that job for the whole war and it wasn't dangerous, so on my second furlough, I got married.
I had met this girl at a dance just before I left and we had been corresponding. You know, you can get quite attached through the mail.
If I'd known I was going to be put in the infantry I would never have married, because you know what happens in a war. There were times we were losing fifty percent a day!
But as it turned out, I did come back, although I had a sixty percent disability. At the time the shrapnel hit my head, they had to operate immediately.
Fortunately, the operation was a success. They didn't cut anything out that was vital. This is one chance in a million.
I'm lucky to be able to speak.

After I got back, my wife and I really got to know each other. But our marriage was not so good in the beginning.
See, when you go in the service, you're programmed to be a soldier. And when you're discharged, you're not de-programmed. You come out a nervous wreck.
After all that fighting, and all of a sudden you've got your freedom. You have to get a job. It's such a vast change.
Anyway, by this time we had a child, and then there was another one. I said to my wife, "I can't live like this and I won't leave you with two children." I had a shop then at Thirteenth and Arch repairing shoes. I was so nervous: everything upset me.
I was ready for a breakdown. So I went to a psychiatrist. He was excellent. A wonderful man. The Veterans' Administration sent me and they paid for it.
I went to him for two years and he helped me to think more clearly—to function, really. He helped me straighten out . . . cope.

You know, there was quite a Jewish community in Kensington.
In the thirty hundred block and on up there were many shops. They were all Jewish stores and the owners lived behind them. In the front was the store and their house was in back.
I remember a very expensive dress shop, Zigelbaum's.
Kensington has always been an industrial section—mostly tapestry and stocking factories.

The workers used to come from Germany mostly. That's how I picked up German. They worked in the factories around us and used to come into our shoe repair shop. Speaking Jewish, which is fourteenth century German, I could understand them.
There was no community life for us, though.
The Gentiles were prejudiced against us. They called each other by their first names, but I was always Mr. Berg. Always formal.
The Jewish shopkeepers looked down on us, too, because we were poor.
Shoemaking did not equate with shopkeeping.
My mother would never go to the synagogue. She felt the women looked down on her. It's true. They were not friendly.
I would have liked to have been a professional.
I was really held back too much. I had the intellect for it. I had the will—the desire—but when I got married—the children—it was too late.

My father died of a heart attack in 1955.
I was very much devoted to my mother, so I said I'd sell the shop in town and take over my father's shop and see what I could do. It was very run down.
It took two years for me to really turn the business around. Now I have more business than I can handle.

We've been here twenty-eight years.
My girl was widowed at twenty-four and left with one child.
My boy still lives with us. He has been going to a neurologist for what I see as emotional problems. He can't seem to work at anything.
I, myself, have come to terms.
I guess I would say music is my greatest pleasure. I have a fine collection of violin records.
The wife and I take little trips, to the mountains, Atlantic City.
I would really like to visit Israel. There's something about that country that fascinates me.
You know, I think if I ever did go there, I wouldn't come back.

Lena Sandberg
Meat Store Manager

I was born on Frankford Avenue in Kensington. 1902.
That makes me seventy-seven.
My parents were born in Russia. They were married and had four children already before they came here. They came with four children and my grandmother.
They had always wanted to make their home in America, the land of gold. They had heard so much about it.
I don't think they had much trouble getting out, then. My mother had a brother here in the second-hand furniture business. He vouched for her.
They came to Kensington and my father opened up a shoe store. In the back of the store he had a little room where he mended shoes, too. He was a real craftsman.
The store was at 2908 Kensington Avenue.
That was called "Jew Town."
There was a kosher meat market, a drug store, a dry goods,
a hardware,
a lot of beautiful stores.

They had a real little community there.
We were religious. Mother lit the candles on Friday nights. But we kept the store open on Saturdays. We had to. That was our busy day, see. They all stayed open on Saturday. We had good business then. At night, in the summertime, after the stores would all be closed, we used to sit outside the store on the sidewalk. Everybody would. We'd bring out our folding chairs and all the neighbors would get together and talk. It was really nice. They were good to each other.

I remember we lived next door to a fruit store. Their name was Soltroff.
One time there was a big trolley strike. I was a little girl, but I can still visualize it. People were throwing stones at a trolley that was passing by our store. I guess they were "for" the strikers and "against" the trolley running.
Mrs. Soltroff saw everybody else throwing stones and she began doing it too. She got so excited she ran across the street and she got run over. She was killed!
I remember my father was the one who ran out and picked her up and carried her into her store.
We all helped her husband after that because her children were still young.
Her sister came from Europe a while later, and she and Mr. Soltroff got married.

We had two synagogues in our neighborhood. One was called "Blocks" and one was called "Brenners." We went to Brenners.
All our neighbors were Jewish. We stayed to ourselves.
I feel there was resentment against us—among the Gentile people—because we had the stores. That's why they called our little area "Jew Town."
We had a good life there, all together. We were not well-off, but we weren't struggling. If I wanted a new dress, I could have it.
We didn't have, what you would call, any real trouble. There were some incidents, but we didn't bother about it.
One time, my brother Morris was studying for his bar mitzvah and father contracted for the rabbi to come to the house certain nights to teach him.
The rabbi was very orthodox. He wore a long black coat and he had a long beard.
One night, some tough Irish kids waylaid him. They caught him at our corner and set his beard on fire!
After that he was afraid to come to our house. But father finally convinced him to come back.

My father would go over to his house and walk him all the way over to our store.
Nobody bothered my father.

Lillie Rovner was my best friend.
Her parents had a notion store right across the street from us.
We walked to school together, studied together, and helped our parents in the stores on Saturdays. I didn't always feel like working on Saturdays, but I did it.
I respected my parents. Whatever they said was *it*. I feared them—like God.
Every Sunday, mother would give me a nickel for working in the store.
Lillie and I used to go to Breyer's Ice Cream Parlor and have a plate of ice cream.
Imagine that! You could go and sit down in style and have a plate of ice cream for a nickel!

We had a good life living there above the shoe store.
At Passover time, mother would make up the seder table right in the store because there was more room there.
She'd pull down the blinds and light the candles. Right there in the store we'd be. We really enjoyed it.
Father was religious—went to synagogue.
The men sat downstairs and we women had to sit up in the balcony. We didn't care. We talked among ourselves while the service was going on downstairs.

Those years growing up in Kensington, the snowstorms were very severe. Yet we used to walk out a lot.
Lillie and I used to take long walks every night.
Before I went to work I spent a lot of time with my mother.
She needed me.
I went out once in a while, but not much.
I was a shy girl. Quiet. I never married.

My father was just marvelous. Tall, good-looking, with a mustache.
He died so young. Only forty-seven.
He was so lovely. Everything for the children. So devoted.
About a year before I went to work, he decided to have his gall bladder out.
Something went wrong. He died. They said he died of "complications." Who knows in them days?

I went to work in the Girard Beef Company, and that's it. I've been there sixty years.
I started as cashier, then bookkeeper, and now I do anything that needs doing. I make up orders. I grind meat. I can carve a side of beef if I have to.
I work seven days a week. Sundays I quit around one.
The owner who hired me is dead now. His children run it, and I'm still there. Like a fixture.
I like my work. There's people around me all the time.
I live alone otherwise.

I don't want you to think I'm lonely.
We were a big family and I have a lot of nieces and nephews. I feel welcome in their homes.
If I could have a wish for the future, it would be to have my family around me all the time. I wouldn't want anything else. That, and to keep working.

William Hartley
Carpet Weaver—Piano Player in Silent Movies

I was born in Yorkshire, Halifax, to be exact. That was in the West-Riding of England. 1892.
My parents worked in an immense carpet factory called Corssleys. It was a big firm, was Corssleys.
He was knighted! His full name was Sir Saville Brinton Corssley.

My father was a carpet weaver. That's how I come to get into it. And *his* father worked at Corssley's Mills. He was an "over-looker." In other words, a "boss."
My mother's father worked in the stone quarries. On the top, though. He used to get aggravated when they'd call him a "delfer." He always reminded them he didn't work down in the delfs. He worked on top! He was a stone mason.

I went to the public school 'til I was eight.
I was going to school when Queen Victoria died.
I remember our teacher, Mr. Maud. Before school started we always

used to sing, "God Save the Queen," and one morning he says to us, "Boys," (we was all boys there) "tomorrow you don't say 'Queen' anymore. From now on it will be 'God Save the King.'"

About a week later, they gave all us boys a bronze medal as big as half a dollar which had a picture of Queen Victoria on it. They gave all us children one.

Father came to this country before us. Things was bad at the time. Very bad. So he left and came to America.

He got a job doing the same thing he done before, out at James and John Dobson's, at the Falls of Schuylkill.

My mother's sister was living here in Kensington and he boarded with them.

He made enough to send for my mother and I, and the little newborn baby that he had never seen.

We come over first class on the American Line Steam Ship. The bill for the three of us was sixty dollars!

I went to school out in the Falls.

That's where Grace Kelly was born, you know.

Jack Kelly and I were pals together. I was Protestant and Jack was Catholic. He should have been going to the Visitation School on Midvale Ave. But the Kellys were poor at that time and he couldn't afford to go to Catholic school.

The result was, in my little school, Jack was sitting right in front of me. We knew each other well.

His brother—the "Virginia Judge," Walter Kelly—was a vaudeville star. I don't know whether you ever heard of him.

Well, he worked as a creel boy in Dobson's Mills, in the carpet department, and he run away from home.

He went down south. While he was down south, he used to go to hear this particular judge pass out sentences every morning.

He could imitate any sort of dialect perfect. Italian, Jewish—no matter what. He was an expert, was Walter. So he went into vaudeville. He was billed as the "Virginia Judge." RCA Victor made records of him.

He even went to London and the queen came to see him in Albert Hall! I know a lot of his funny stories.

Then there was the other brother. The one that won the Pulitzer Prize with his novel, *Craig's Wife.* That was George Kelly.

Here's what a lot of people doesn't know about George. Walter and Grace's father, they were athletes. Real athletes! Real robust. But George was kind of quiet and timid.

People doesn't know this. Being we was all kids together, I remember. George, being so different from the other brothers, he got the nickname of "Sissy Kelly." And he won the Pulitzer Prize!

The school I went to in the Falls of Schuylkill was called the Forrest School.
I didn't go there long because I was working in Dobson's Mills when I was thirteen, full time.
That was an immense factory, was Dobson's. He manufactured velvets, carpets, blankets.
I was supposed to be fourteen. They told fibs in those days. It was the common thing to get the kids working.
What I did was put my two front fingers on the spool of a "mule" and give it a twist. The machinery ran back and forth and spun the yarn. You might say the machinery done the rest. That was my first job.
I was thirteen.

Old John Dobson, he used to walk through the mill. Old John. He and his brother, they came from England and they talked real broad. Why you'd think they'd just got off the boat!
He was a queer sort of bird, was John. Like, they were millionaires at the time, and we used to see him on Allegheny Avenue, and if he saw a little nut or a nail, he'd pick it up and put it in his pocket.
Out there in his factory he was getting robbed right and left! Stealing this! Stealing that! Nuts and bolts by the million! Yet he'd see one on the street and pick it up.
I remember, working there in his factory, you had to watch out for Old John. He was tricky, he was.
He'd come up to a new boy working on his machine and he'd take out his cigar and he'd say, "Got a match?"
If the boy went in his pockets and handed him a match he'd say, "Pack up your things. You're fired!"
See, you wasn't supposed to smoke in the factory. The poor boy. Here he was aiming to please and he was fired.
But what would happen was, the boy would go to his foreman to tell him, and the foreman would tell him to go home and come back to work in a day or two. There was so many boys, Old John wouldn't know the difference.
I left Dobson's at seventeen and went over to Down's Mills on Indiana Street. It was owned by three old ladies, but while I was there they sold it to Tommy Devlin real cheap.
It's idle now. They made very good carpets. Wiltons, they was called. I went there as a creel boy, as you had to be twenty-one to run a loom.

It was piece work, of course. I never worked anything else.
Neither did my wife. She worked at Quaker Lace Company. She worked there fifty-four years, winding.
She kind of liked it and it was steady. Even during the Depression she could count on a few days a week. That's why she stayed.
Her parents came from Belfast. They were steady people.
At the time that I met her, I was quite a sport. I had this lovely Studebaker car.
That was fifty years ago. At that time, very few people had cars. You could park anywhere.
Well, I worked with her father. He was the same as me, a carpet weaver.
Anyway, at that time of our lives, a little gang that we had used to gather at each other's houses for parties. We were all young then. We had parties every Sunday night. Clean, respectable parties they were. I was working with this fellow named Carter, and this particular time he says to me, "We're having a party at our house tonight if you want to come down."
An' I says, "I got to go."
An' he says, "Whoever you're going with, bring 'em down."
So there was a lot of girls out there. We didn't go steady with 'em. But we all knew each other. An' I had this girl, so I brought her down to Carter's house.
When supper was put out, I was sitting opposite this other one. I knew her father. An' I kept looking at her.
I found she only lived around the corner from me!
Course the girl I had with me, she didn't mind. We weren't—you know, we were just pals. That's all.
So, it was summertime, and people sat on their front doorsteps then. I thought, "Oh, she'll be sitting on her doorstep." I must have driven around her block twenty times!
Sure enough, one of the trips 'round, there she was . . . sitting. I stopped and said, "Hello!" (Nothing new under the sun, is there?)
Well, I got out and her father saw me. He knew me, mind you.
I was no spring chicken, as you might say. I was thirty-five. We were married 1927.

A year or two after that, the Depression hit us. We was all out of work. No work for us at our mill. No work anywhere!
People stayed where they was, though, because if any work did come in, you knew you'd be called, if only for a few days. You waited for the call.
Then, there was no such thing as unemployment or welfare.

You were on your own.
Downtown they had a program where they gave you free soap to sell.
I didn't have the carfare to ride downtown, so I used to walk.
Seven miles it was.
They gave you a cardboard box with soap and a sign to wear on your hat. It said, "Unemployed." I wouldn't wear the sign and I'd hide my soap in a briefcase. They wouldn't come to the door if they saw the box and the sign.
I'd walk all the way down, get the soap, and wind my way back home. And the result would be maybe seventy-five cents. Half of 'em wouldn't even come to the door.
Quaker Lace, where my wife worked, called her in two or three days most weeks, though, so we managed.

About this time I decided to try to pick up a little extra money playing the organ in the silent movies.
I always loved music. I had a natural ability for it. I remember when I was a boy in the Falls, I used to pester my poor parents for a piano.
I wanted a piano more than anything in this world!
Well, they weren't rich, you know, so they went to this second-hand store on the Ridge, and they bought this old flat top with four legs to it. A real antique it were. All out of tune. They paid ten dollars. It was in the parlor. They wanted to surprise me.
I come home and they say, in broad Yorkshire dialect,
"Hey, William! Go it to parlor and see wots there!"
I open the door and they call out,
"William has got his piana!"
I started to play it. Oh! It sounded like a bunch of tin cans. Half the keys wouldn't go down.
We had a boarder then and he says,
"Never mind, William, ge' it tuned."
I found a tuner down on the Ridge. He wanted two dollars to tune it, but when he looks at it, he informs me it wasn't worth it. It laid there in the parlor 'til we moved, and then—we left it there.
Anyway, to get back, I used to go in my spare time to the YMCA.
They had a big organ there. You could practice on it for a dollar an hour. No teacher. You were on your own. You had a hard time getting that hour, too, because anyone who could play was hoping to get a job playing for the silent movies.
My wife knew the usher at the Eagle Theater on Kensington Avenue. She got me the job, really. I started out as a relief player on Saturdays. It was hard work. I started 11:30 in the morning, and I'd play right through to the last show that night.

They gave you the music plan to follow. It was fitted to the picture, see. Five minutes of fight scene music. Five minutes of love scene music. If the action was, say, in South America, you played Spanish style music.
You had to follow the cue sheet. If you went off and played on your own, say a popular song, all the audience would start to hum or sing to it. So you couldn't do that.
I got so I played at other theaters, too. Relief work. After a while, I got so good I did my own composing. I could imitate the sound of an airplane even.

When things picked up, I got a steady job weaving again.
On weekends, I'd play at the theaters. Say, we had some good times then!
When I'd get through playing, Edna would meet me and we'd go over to Matthew's Oyster House. There's no more restaurants like that anymore. Oysters were thirty-five cents a dozen. Big ones! We'd have oysters and beer. Sometimes with friends. We'd get to feeling good and toast each other.
You know, the old time Yorkshire workers were a cheerful bunch. I remember one toast this friend of mine used to make—used to make us all laugh:
"Here's to me, and my wife's husband, not forgetting myself!"
Matthew's had a lovely dining room and an elegant oyster saloon. Magistrates and judges ate there!
Dr. Guinette, the famous singing dentist, would come there after his concerts. Big hat. Curly hair. He had a voice like Caruso. He used to sing at the People's Theater. When he sang "My Hero" from *The Chocolate Soldier,* they came down the aisle with roses for him.

We never had children. But we raised plenty!
My sister's husband died and left her with nine. We had the kids over to our place every night for years.
Because she was a widow, her minister wanted her to put the boys in Girard College, but she wouldn't. She wanted them home with her. We helped out.

We've lived on this street now for forty years.
The last twenty-seven years of my working life I was at Archibald Holmes Carpet Mills, and I get a pension now every month from them.
What with Social Security, owning our home and being in good health, we just stay on here.

In the old country, they used to say,
"Every day will be Sunday by and by."
Being retired, it does seem like every day's a holiday. We enjoy ourselves, go downtown for dinners. It's surprising when you're out what you can find to do.
I don't play the piano anymore, though. There's an old saying,
"Music is a jealous suitor. You leave it. It leaves you."
If things would stay the same here as they were, we would be content.

Trio:
"Aunt Sadie"
Textile Burler and Mender

Up at Craftex, they all called me "Aunt Sadie."
Two of my nieces are still working there now, Jean McNight and Dolores. I got them their jobs.
My nephew helps Mr. Brown in the shipping department today. So everybody who works here now—they still call me "Aunt Sadie" when I come in. That's all I ever got for years.
Dolores' sister-in-law works at Craftex too. I worked there for twenty-one years.

I'm seventy-eight years old. I was born on Kipp Street in Kensington. My mother came from England. Father too.
We're Catholic.
Father worked in a dye house. Mother never worked. My father was very strict, but we loved him. We always respected them both.
We're four children living. Four dead.

For a few years we lived up in the coal-mining district, for my
mother's health. She had to get out of Kensington, the doctor told my
father.
We had aunts and uncles up in Carbondale, Pennsylvania. So we
moved up there for a few years.
I used to sled down them big hills up there.
In the wintertime, we used to go out in the coal fields and pick coal.
Come back with as much as you could carry.
In the summer, we picked berries. It was all sport for us. We loved it.
My father wanted to come back, though, and as soon as our mother
got to feeling better, he moved us back to Kensington.
He was working on the railroad up there but he didn't want to stay.

I worked in textiles from the time I came back here.
I was fourteen and very grown-up.
My mother nearly had a fit because I wouldn't go back to school.
I wanted to be like everybody else. I wanted to work.
Well, we children had come down to Kensington a few weeks ahead of
our mother. She had to wait up there for the freight to take our
furniture.
We stayed at my aunt's. So I got this job and went right to work.
By the time she got down, I had four pays waiting for her.
Four pays of my own to give her.
She was so mad because I was in the eighth grade, and she wanted me
to go back to school. She was glad to get the four pays, but still she
said she was disappointed I didn't go to school.

I went into an underwear place on Ontario Street. Akiff Underwear.
My job was to put the ribbon through the shirts.
Remember when they used to wear the underwear with the little pink
ribbon through the shirt? That's what I did.
Then I went into a cloth mill. Walthers, on Torresdale Avenue.
I was a specker. That's picking the white specks out of the cloth.
Then Mr. Walthers took twelve of us upstairs to learn mending.
I've been mending ever since.
But those days you worked from seven in the morning to quarter to
six at night. Saturdays, half a day.
That was in 1925. There was good money in mending then.
That's the truth.
Well, when Walthers got slack, they laid us off.
A friend of mine, Ada Stronzlo, got me a job at Craftex Mills. She
still works there on the second shift.

Craftex needed cloth menders at the time because they had gotten some government work.

I worked on the second shift and then they made me floorlady on the third shift until I retired.

I really liked the third shift. I'll tell you why. You have more time for yourself during the day.

With the second shift you don't. You know, second shift you work three-thirty to twelve. And really, by the time you get home and go to bed, and by the time you get up . . . you have no time! It's just get your breakfast, go to the stores, do your housework and get supper ready and then, it's go to work! You don't have enough time to yourself.

The first shift is all right but I couldn't get on it at first. Too much seniority ahead of me.

It never seemed to bother me—third shift. When I'd go home, I wouldn't eat breakfast. I'd go right to bed.

Took me half an hour to get home. The buses were running good in them days. I'd get home seven-thirty A.M. and go right to bed. I'd sleep 'til eleven or twelve.

I had five boys and one daughter, but by the time I was working third shift, they were pretty well grown.

Well, I'd get up about twelve and I'd go and do my errands and my housework. Then I'd get supper ready. I had lots of time to myself.

Craftex is the only place I ever worked that had shifts, which I think is very good for working mothers.

If one of my boys was sick, I would take him to my sister's. She lived near me.

But to tell you the truth, I can never say I spent a dollar on a doctor for any of my children. They were all healthy, every one of them.

They were all breast-fed babies, and when they were very little, I used to always leave them in a nursery where they took care of children of working mothers—kept them all day.

There was one right near me, across from Diamond Street Square. Sacred Heart Day Nursery.

They kept them from seven in the morning until I could stop for them at night. It didn't bother me much. I never had any trouble with any of them.

I married when I was twenty-three. He was a Kensington boy.
But I left him when my youngest was three.
He couldn't seem to work. He was a spoiled boy, you know?

An only child.
I wouldn't go on relief, or anything like that.
So I thought, "Here. I've got to go to work."
I thought to myself, "If I'm going to work, I'll work for my children. Not him."
You know, that man could do anything. Any kind of work.
But he never hardly worked!
He wanted to be a white-collar man. He liked to be dressed up all the time.
So I raised the six children myself from when the youngest was three years old.
I never bothered with a divorce.
He's dead now.

Talking about the good times, when we were seventeen or eighteen, our Sunday nights would be spent walking.
We'd walk all the way over Allegheny Avenue to Broad Street and come back.
Everybody would be dressed up and out walking. It was like a parade in them days. People would get dressed up and everybody would walk over the avenue and back.
That was a regular Sunday night affair. It was really nice. I often think of that. You wouldn't think of doing that now! And we used to go to dances. Danceland. Wagners. The Oaks. On Saturday nights, everybody danced.
Of course, with my father, you had to be home a certain time. We darsn't stay out after twelve o'clock! When that dance was over, we had to go home.
Now my mother was just the opposite.
She'd say, "Look, as long as I know where they are, I'll never worry. They always tell me where they are. They never lie to me."
But my father, he thought when you worked you should be in bed early. He used to go to bed early every night and he'd be to work before they opened the place.
He thought we should do the same thing.

We had good times as kids.
Jacks, roller skates, jump rope.
But the best I liked was up in Carbondale. Sledding, picking coal.
I thought it was wonderful. I didn't have to go out with the coal-pickers. I wanted to.
You wanted to beat the next one, how much you could bring home.

I loved it. We'd pull the coal home on sleds or wagons, or whatever we had at the time.
In the summer, we'd pick berries. We'd start with the strawberries and go right through to the blackberries. Oh, I loved it!
I still go there to visit. My sister can't understand it.
She says, "I never long for it."
I says, "I do."

I worked hard all my life.
I never regretted it. I had a good life.
I never think of things I might of done different.
When I learned mending, I really liked it. They used to laugh at me. They'd say they never heard tell of anybody loving their work, but I'd say, "I do."
The hours were long in those days. You'd think you were never going to be done work. You know?
And then, working on Saturday seven to twelve—Saturday night you'd be tired out. Wouldn't feel like going out.
But we still would. We'd still go to our dances.

When I retired, I worked part time in a grocery store. It was small, more like a delicatessen.
A friend of mine had it and he asked me if I would help him out.
So I says, "Well, part time,"
and he says, "All right."
I worked there for quite a while. I enjoyed it because I had never done anything like that.
Then I come back to Craftex for two years. I was sixty-eight when I come back. I didn't stop 'til I was seventy.
And guess what? I was going to go back last year! Because I find now that it's really hard to get along on Social Security.
But I got called for jury duty and that settled that.
And then the winter come and I won't go out in the ice. I fell two years ago on the ice.
But if they called me today, I would go back. I could use the money.
And I miss the friends. I have a lot of friends still send me cards at Christmas from all the years I worked with them.
I had some nice friends. I always got along with everybody.
I was never afraid of crime, but lately I am.
We live in the Thirty-first Ward on the east side of Front Street.
There's a few Blacks and Puerto Ricans moved in on Front Street, but on the other side. There's no Blacks in the Thirty-first Ward yet.

But you know, over on Hope Street, little Hope Street, they had colored living there for years. And no one, as long as ever I can remember, ever had any trouble. Never.
The only ones I ever knew were at work, and they were always very nice to me. But now, I'm more afraid.
Still, I wouldn't move. I'm getting too old.
We have a nice street. They're small homes, but they're well kept.

When I lived on Tulip Street, there was a German family lived across from us. And do you know, any time there was ever any kind of celebration for the Germans, they used to have one of those old-fashioned German bands come and play outside their door.
A real German band! Oh, it was so cute. Like, for a birthday, a little German band would come and play in the street. Oh, it was so nice! We used to enjoy that.
I used to laugh at my father. He lived with me for two years before he died.
You know, the Polish used to have a band lead their funeral processions. A real Polish band would lead everybody up and down the streets.
One day, one was passing by our house playing away. Father was standing at the front window.
"When I die," he says to me, "that's what I want. I want a band!"
He was English, you know. We used to laugh at him. Every time one went by he'd say,
"That's the greatest thing I ever heard tell!"
I was close to my father in spite of his strictness. He was a great man. A lot of fun.
I didn't resent any of my childhood or growing up, except for my husband. That was all.
I had a nice family. I raised a nice family.
I have twenty-two grandchildren and three great-grandchildren. Another one on the way.
My sons Vinnie and Joey, when they were younger, used to work for Craftex in the mending room, carrying the cuts.

All the kids are married now. Have their own families, except for my daughter.
She had a nervous breakdown in 1952 and she never rightly come out of it.
She's smart. You wouldn't want to see a smarter girl in your life. There isn't nothing she can't talk to you about.
She went through high school and all. But she quit. Just like that.

She lives at home with me. She'll be fifty-two in July.
I guess after I go, the boys will take care of her. Oh, yes.
They always said that. "Never worry about her."
The boys all went in the service and when they come out, they all went into different jobs.
Billy's a policeman.
George was a police officer, but he got stabbed pretty bad. He's on disability now.

They call me "Aunt Sadie" on my street, too.
See, I was married on my street, where I live now, and everybody knows me.
The only thing I feel bad about Kensington is, all those factories that moved out.
Just look at this factory next door. Just a shell. Burnt down. The one next to that. That's out.
In fact, in Kensington there used to be nothing but textile. Hosiery.
A while back there were all hosiery mills. Now it's nothing.
They're empty.
Years ago a lot of them moved away. Hosiery went out of business.
A lot of people lost their jobs.
The same way with cloth. There's only a couple of small cloth places left. It's really a shame.
But I won't move. No way. I'll stay where I'm at. I'm contented.
I like it.
And it's handy for everything. It's handy for the buses and all.
I can take the Five, or the Three, or the Fifty-seven, or the El.
I'm within a block of everything.
If I got sick, my neighbors would help if I needed them. But my nieces and nephews would help, too.
We have a big family and we have a close family. We're very close.
Every one of us.

Nancy McCoy
Forelady of a Textile Burling and Mending Room

I was raised on Water Street.
Well, you know about down here. The neighbors are better to you, sometimes, than your own family. If you have trouble, they're right there.
There's people on my street that has been there from when I was a child, and they're still there.
My mother's friends are still there. They're the ones my brother still visits.
When my brother was in his teens it seemed he was always getting into trouble. You know, with the gangs and the fighting?
So my mother made up her mind to move out of Kensington. For his sake. She moved up north, and after she moved—my brother came back every weekend to be with the same crowd. And he's still coming! He's married and has children and a big home and a good job—and he still comes down to Kensington to see his friends. They were raised together, and they're very close.
When Betty, my daughter, moved up to the northeast, she cried.

She wanted to move back.
First of all, she was never that far away from me.
Second, they was all hoity-toity up there.
There was no avenue to shop and she didn't drive.
When she got to know her neighbors, she found a lot of them were people who had moved out of Kensington themselves.
There wasn't much difference. There was still fist fights in the street occasionally. Arguments over the kids.

My father was in the trucking business. He had a trucking concern right off of Kensington Avenue. The business was his father's originally.
In fact, Alice Dorsey who works here with me, her husband used to drive one of my father's trucks. Small world.
Father had seventeen trucks at one time. It was a big business.
Around 1941, he went bankrupt. He lost everything.
His brother, who was in the business with him, was suffering from cancer, and they spent a lot of money trying to save him.
My first husband used to say to me,
"The only reason I married you is because your father had seventeen trucks."
That's the truth. Anyway, he lost it all.
After that, he opened up a fruit stand at Front and York. But the competition from the big markets was too much. He got depressed about it.
Mom went to work and began to take care of everything. She used to say, "The paper boy makes more money than you."
In 1946, he had a heart attack. He was sick a long time. In fact, he never worked again.
Mom started work as a mender in Craftex Mills. I came in to work with her when I was eighteen.
She taught me. I taught my daughter.
I showed my daughter all the things my mother taught me.

My father was a quiet person.
I don't know if he minded my mother going to work. He didn't seem to.
She always feared he was going to drop over with another heart attack.
We were always told, "Your father might not be here next year."
Every holiday we had to go home and have holiday dinners there because,
"Your father might not be here next year."

And mom died before my father, with a heart attack. See what I mean? She died suddenly—within a few minutes. She went in to take a shower this one night and came out and fell over.
He was very lost without her. He lived alone but he was always down at my place with me. Always with me. I took care of him. I cooked for him, every meal.
He took sick in my house. Mom died in 1970 and he died in 1971. They would have been married fifty years.
Actually, I felt he died of a broken heart. The only fighting I remember was over gambling. Father's card games. Constant card games. And the constant fighting about it. My father was a compulsive gambler.
I think when he lost his business is when he took his heart attack. He was sick a long time.
That's when my mother went out to work.
Mother was Irish Catholic, and my father was an Orthodox Jew. There was no fighting over religion. Gambling, yes. Religion, no. That is, they didn't care but their families did. Her family disowned her. She didn't see her people for years.
She had one brother that was dead three years and she didn't even know it. And another sister that was dead two years!
They never bothered with her. On account of that, she was fairly close to his father. The mother, no—but grandfather accepted.
Father was a quiet man. Never said too much. If it hadn't been for his gambling, there wouldn't have been any arguments.
My father's parents must have been well off, but I don't remember them helping financially. I just remember us struggling.

We went to a little Baptist church because it was near us. Then we started going to Saint Luke's which was High Episcopalian.
I have sisters that have turned Catholic now. But mother didn't bring us up in the church. She always said when we were old enough we could turn, if we wanted to.
She was more or less in favor of it. She herself was religious.
She always had her rosaries out and she was always praying.
My sister works here with me now. She turned Catholic and she raised her children Catholic. She needed to.
But I was satisfied just going to Saint Luke's. I had my children christened High Episcopalian.
Father used to say he didn't care what church we went to as long as we had religion in our hearts.
Mother felt the same way. She always used to say,

"There's just one God."
So there was never no tension over that.
So, I don't remember fighting over religion, just over his gambling.

I quit high school when I was sixteen and went to a technical school.
I took up commercial, stenography and typing.
But after a few months, I realized I could make more money in factory work, so I quit and took a job in a spinning mill.
I was making more money as a twister in a spinning mill than my sister who graduated commercial and was working in an office.
When I was eighteen, I got pregnant and had to quit for a while.
When I went back to work, mom got me a job with her in the mending department at Craftex.

My husband worked at Stetson Hats. He was a shrinker. I remember his hands always being sore from the hot water.
I met him in the Kent Movie House. There was movie houses all around then. I was fourteen years old. He was seventeen.
Then he went into the service during the war. When he came out, we got married. He was twenty. I was sixteen, going on seventeen.
I loved him.
If it hadn't been for his drinking problem and our daughter dying, I think we would be together today.
I always loved him. I just couldn't stand the drinking. He'd go very belligerent when he drank and it was rough.
You never knew from week to week if he was going to bring home any pay. That's why I always worked.
I was working the second shift when my second little girl, Nancy, swallowed a charm. Ruptured her esophagus. She was ill for thirteen months before she died.
She was in the hospital—that happened on December fifteenth—and she came out February eighth.
Then she was an out-patient. It was rough. We had to take her back every day for treatment. She had to be fed through her stomach.
He idolized her. And afterwards, we couldn't do nothing with him.
Then he came down very sick.
She died on a Saturday. We buried her on Wednesday.
That Friday night he came in doubled up. He had ruptured ulcers that broke into the wall of his pancreas. He was in the hospital sixty-eight days.
They told him never to drink again. And he's still alive today, and he's an alcoholic!

This is what amazes me. She would be twenty-seven now. She died when she was five. So you figure, this man has still been drinking for twenty-two more years!
You wonder sometimes. How can this man live? Before he was just, you know . . . but he became very violent afterwards.
I was doctoring Betty, my oldest girl, for nerves at eight years old. And it was through him.
So that's what made me leave. Her.
If I didn't have my mother, I don't know what I would have done. My mother was always there when I needed her. 'Til the day she died, she was there. With all of us. She'd come and borrow off of one to give to the other.
She always worked, too. She had a hard life with my father because of the gambling. And then, he didn't work. He didn't work for years on account of his heart, you know.
So I went back to live with mom—me and Betty.
Mom got me a job at Craftex Mills on the third shift with her at first. I was twenty-seven.
It just seems like my life has been nothing but working.
Sometimes I get so tired. And I think it's more from my nervous system today because I have a teenager now by my second marriage. I mean, with Betty I didn't worry. But with the drugs and the things that's out there today that they're facing, it scares me.
My little one is going to vocational school next year. She wants to take up cosmetology, passed the test for it. They took twenty out of two hundred! She was picked. I was happy about that. Just hope she makes it.
These kids today, I'm telling you. It's rough. It really is. You don't know what they're facing out there. It's rough in the schools. I think this is why so many children are quitting. It's too rough for them in the schools with the drugs and the tensions and the racial problems and the gangs.
You know? This is what it is, and it's in all the schools. It's not just in Kensington. Believe me. They have it up in the northeast too. They have it all over. In the high schools, it's really getting bad, the drugs. And I feel a lot of these children . . .
that's why the parents go along with them, letting them quit. I feel I'll let my daughter quit. Yes, I will.
I've seen what some of these parents have went through with these children that has got in trouble in these high schools. I feel, rather than go through that, I'd let her quit.
Drug addicts, gangs, tensions and fear. These children go to school in fear today. They can't squeal on one another. They're not allowed to tell on anyone. They'd get beat up so bad.

I remember, years ago, we never owned a key. We never locked the door!
Today, you wouldn't go to the store without locking the door because of the robberies, and a lot of the younger kids on drugs break in to get money for their habit.
You're scared to walk the streets. I remember, as a child, walking out two, three o'clock in the morning. I would walk down to the avenue with the rest of them.
Today you wouldn't dare do that. Fear.

I'm looking forward to retirement. Just to sit back.
I just hope I'm not like my mother. She was supposed to go up and sign for Social Security in April. She died in March. She never collected a day of her Social Security. She raised a big family. Worked all her life. She was sixty-five when she died. She worked on a Friday night and died on Sunday.

Really, I don't have no time for hobbies. When I go home, I cook supper.
And after supper I do the washing and cleaning around the house. Then I cook supper again for my husband. He works second shift. He's a diabetic and has to have a hot meal. He's in charge of shipping at Craftex at night. He never knows what time he can take off for supper. It all depends when the trucks come in. He'll call and I'll have his meal ready and out. It's a rush job for him, too. He eats on the fly.

When we retire, I'd like to take a trip. To Florida. I've never been there. Florida or Hawaii.
Maybe after our youngest gets married. My husband and I have never had a honeymoon. Never had one the first time. So after this one gets married, I feel as though we could take a trip. She's fifteen and talking about getting married. She has a boyfriend. He's very nice. I'm fond of him. This is it. This is what I hear from her.
"You got married when you were sixteen. Betty got married when she was sixteen."
She don't consider Betty a stepsister. She considers her a sister. They're very close.
Betty was fifteen when our youngest was born. I'm very proud of Betty. She's such a comfort.
This young one will be a comfort, too, when she gets older. It's just a phase she's going through. She's very rebellious. If you punish her she rebels where Betty never did.
I don't remember ever having to holler at Betty. She just listened to what she was told. Never had any trouble, outside of her getting

married too young. And I don't feel that was so terrible. When she wanted to come back, she knew the door was open.

I remember myself going home to my mother. We are following steps, because my mother was like that.

Whenever I had trouble or wanted to come home, the door was open. Mother used to say, "The door opens both ways. You can come in or you can go out."

Really, my mom. I always remember one thing she used to say:

"If everybody's troubles was out on a line, you'd go and pick your own."

And when I get depressed about bills and money, I think of another one she used to say:

"I thought I was poor because I had no shoes, until I seen a man with no feet."

She always—we were raised by those quotations, and I've raised Betty by them. And I even try with the young one.

I feel I've had a troubled life. Sad. With an alcoholic for my first husband.

Losing a daughter like I did.

It's always stuck back in my head. I think it has helped damage the youngest one because I've been a nervous wreck since the day she was born, afraid something would happen to her.

I wouldn't allow her to go in the street. Always scared of accidents. You can't live that way, and it was hard on her.

We protected her and now she's becoming a lady and she don't want you to baby her. And I still baby her. I wait on her. I worry about her. I'm awful. I know it's wrong. I'm finding this out. But it's just that fear all the time.

As my first husband said when we lost Nancy:

"You don't feel as though this is ever going to happen to you. It's only things you read about in the papers."

It's true. Those thirteen months I spent in Children's Hospital, I seen deaths from goofy things. You wouldn't believe. A child falling off a sofa. A cut foot. And they end up losing their lives over it. You know? Things you would never realize. And it has really shook me up seeing those children.

I'm religious. I believe in God. And I pray.

I don't go to church and I'm sorry. I'm thinking about going back.

I went to the High Episcopal Church. When I went to divorce my first husband, I was told the High Episcopals didn't believe in divorce. You wouldn't be able to take communion and such. I don't know.

I think I became bitter when the little girl died. The Father came to see me and I asked questions, and he just couldn't answer them. I often wonder why God took her. I seen all those people in Kensington—in the streets, drinking, out at night—their children left alone and neglected. And I worked so hard to give my children everything. It doesn't seem fair.
And then, to tell me I shouldn't get a divorce! I just turned around and said to the Father, I said, this is what I said to him:
"*You* live with that drunk!" That's just what I said.
And I never went back to that church.

Betty Makarewicz
Textile Burler and Mender

I was born Betty Eichel.
My mother remarried when I was fourteen.
My real father is in Veterans' Hospital right now, dying of alcoholism.
My stepfather, to me, is my father.
We lived at Fourth and York Streets until my mother and father were divorced. They separated when I was nine.
My father had a drinking problem to begin with and then, when we lost my sister, he really went.
Her name was Nancy. She died when she was five years old. I was eight. She swallowed a charm off of her bracelet and it punctured her esophagus.
It was a terrible time for my mother and apparently, my father was weaker. At a time when she needed him, he needed the drink.

My parents were born here in Kensington. When we left my father, we returned to where my mother grew up, to my grandmother's on Water Street.

Mother's father was German Jewish.
Her mother was Irish Catholic.
My grandfather's people had a trucking business which they left to him and his brother. They lost it.
I don't know, truly, whether it was the Depression or what, but I know he had a gambling problem.
In later years, as I remember him, he had a fruit stand down on Front Street. He sold fruit and produce, and at Christmas time, Christmas trees. At Easter Time, Easter plants.
My Irish grandmother was a doll-baby. She's the one that got us all jobs working with her when we needed them.
She worked until the day before she died. She was a mender and she always worked on the third shift, midnight to seven A.M.
When mother and I came to live with her, she got mother a job mending on the second shift.
Actually, mother has always worked. I don't remember minding because she was always there when I needed her. Either she or my grandmother was always there.
My grandmother was like another mother to me. She worked the third shift. Always the third shift. With her seniority, she could have got on first. I don't know if she was just a night person, or what. Grandmother would lay down after dinner and sleep 'til midnight and time for her to go.
But by then, my mother was there. So I always had somebody with me constantly. Either one of the two. I never felt alone or deserted because they were working.
My grandmother got me my job at Craftex mending on the second shift. I was nineteen, separated from my husband, and going through a divorce myself. That's why I had to work.
I was married at sixteen. He was sixteen too. My parents were mad about it, but mother felt if she didn't give her permission, we would of ran away anyway.
I tell her today I don't think I would of had the nerve, but at the time, I was very determined.
Looking back, I really don't know. But I don't regret any of it because I have my daughter.

I met my husband in junior high. Mother took me out after the eighth grade and tried to give me a profession. She sent me to Saint Anne's Commercial. It was private and mother had to pay. I realize now it was a strain on her.
It was a new experience for me, going to a Catholic school. I did fairly well, but the thing I loved about it, believe it or not, was the religious course. I was fascinated by it. It was my best subject. I hung on every

word. I didn't convert to Catholicism, though. I thought a lot about it. I went to instruction at Visitation Church but got frightened off by a priest there and stopped. I really got frightened. I was young and very gullible and he started asking me about confession and—I don't know how to say this; you have to understand this was the first instruction—if I did this with my boyfriend, would I confess it?
He was a very young priest.
I kept saying, "I don't do them things!" You know? I got very upset. This leads me to believe that I wasn't meant to go in that direction or I might have sought someone else and followed up. I never did. Which I don't regret to this day because now I'm following my religion, Episcopalian.

Anyway, I graduated business school with second honors, but I didn't put any of it to use because of getting married so young.
I graduated school in June and (this is the depressing part) turned sixteen in August and got married in October. My little girl was born the following year.
My husband quit school and started working with my stepfather in a storm window factory. He was making terrific money which we didn't realize at the time and just blew it and had a ball.
He had a drinking problem, too.
We didn't stay married, I think, because we were both so young and, you know, in my time sex was a big issue. Today it's much more free, where then you didn't do things like that unless you were married. I'm sure today, where kids don't wait, I might not have gotten married. But the pressure was so great that you didn't do anything. And you were so young and thought you were so much in love that you had to get married. We were both too young.

His family had a drinking problem. His mother had this drinking problem and I didn't realize he was going to follow in his family's footsteps.
I saw it in his mother, and I saw the dislike he had for his mother—which is why he probably wanted to escape and thought that would be enough for him.
But as it turned out, he returned; and because he was too young even to drink in bars, he used to go to his mother's house and drink! And then wouldn't get up for work, and the money wasn't coming in, and it was just . . . plus he was very jealous. An obsession. Really sick kind of jealousy. Nothing normal. So that was . . . and I think, coming from my background, the drinking scared me more than

anything else. I thought, "I'm not going to put up with what my mother put up with for a lot of years."
So I left him and went back to my mother's.

By this time, my mother had married again and had her own home. My stepfather, God bless him, was so patient.
I kept breaking up with my husband and coming home and going back—I must have gone back and forth ten times before I finally decided that was it. He wasn't going to change.
Mother and grandmother got me into Craftex with them as a mender. Mother had married again when I was fourteen. He was a bartender. She was going out at the time. Actually, she was dating the owner of the bar and he was only working there.
After they got married, he gave up bartending because she got pregnant right away. That was really a shock-a-roo because she wasn't expecting it. She hadn't been able to have another baby after my sister died, so she thought she couldn't anymore.
I was thrilled to death. It was like having a doll to take care of.
My mother was upset because they were just starting out and didn't have much. I didn't realize they were having it rough because of the way they are. I never did without anything.
They were paying for my business school too. Finally my stepfather found this job in the storm window place and things got easier.

Once I got working at Craftex, I saved up the money for my divorce. Five hundred dollars for the lawyer. Fifty dollars to take him to court for child support. He didn't pay anyway.
Now my second husband has adopted her. When I first came to work, I asked for the second shift because my mother worked on day shift and grandmother worked on third.
When mother worked during the day I watched our two children because there was only two years difference between my sister and my daughter.
Well, mother would go to work in the morning. I would have the kids during the day. I'd clean up and start dinner.
My grandfather would come down and take over the overlap between my leaving and my mother's coming home. He would sit with the children for that hour.
Mother would come home, start dinner and put the children to bed. I'd get home after midnight.
You're all wound up when you get home, you know. I couldn't always go to bed right away. I wasn't tired. I was nineteen. Sometimes I'd go out with the girls after work.

I lost my teen years. I never really experienced a social life.
So that time when I was free and working was a good time for me.
I had a little bit of independence which I had never known. I enjoyed it. I'd go out after twelve with the girls for a couple of hours. Not every night. Maybe once a week. It was a new experience for me.
We'd go to the taproom on the corner—me, Hattie, Lorraine.
We'd sit around and relax.
I wouldn't get home 'til maybe two o'clock, and then it was up at seven with the kids. It didn't bother me.
I took the bus home from work sometimes, but mostly my grandfather would bring my grandmother into work, and then he would take me home. If we went to the taproom, one of the girls would drive me.

I met my second husband at work. He worked for Synthetic Finishing Company. He was the driver.
When the truck would come to pick up the rolls, he would come back to my table. We'd talk. He had been married before, divorced, and lost a child.
I sort of related to him because of my mother. His name was Bill Makarewicz. He's Polish, another non-practicing Catholic.
We were married in church, but I have since had our marriage blessed by an Episcopalian minister because I started my religion again.
He's older than I am.
My daughter was young and I think it represented a little bit of security for me, because going out is all right for a while but then you get tired.
He had bought a new home, and he was very good to my daughter.
In the meantime, her real father had stopped supporting her, which I let go because I was working and I would rather he didn't see her because of his drinking.
Her name is Anna Madeliene. We call her Nancy.
Now I have another daughter. Patricia is eight. Nancy is thirteen.
They're both in school now, so the bigger one watches, gets the little one off in the mornings.
Bill and I leave the house together at ten of seven. He still works at Synthetic Finishing Company.
Now he's a machine operator. He's been there twenty years.

So, things have leveled off for me.
Looking back over my childhood, with all the troubles—Nancy dying, the divorce—you would think I would remember being sad, but I don't.

I had a wonderful relationship with my mother. And I loved my grandmother.

On summer nights and after school we played street games. I had a lot of friends on the street. We played "Hop-scotch," "Freedom," "Swing-the-belt." We used to play "Jacks" when I was younger, on our steps. I can remember scrubbing the white steps which we don't have anymore. We used to have—every Saturday you had to get out there with a brush. That was my job. We all had jobs.

We jumped rope. "Double-Dutch." We were big on "Monopoly" at one time. And a game called "Concentration." We used to sit on our front steps and play it.

And then, as I got older, we more or less just stood around the corners, hanging out. Boys and girls together. We acted tough but we weren't, really. Going to Stetson Junior High, you had to act tough to survive.

As we got a lot older, we listened to records at one another's houses. Mooned over boys.

I always had the freedom to bring my friends to our house at any time. We could always have our parties, or get together at my place, even though they were all working at the time.

I didn't realize how much it was on them. It was always my steps we congregated on because my folks were so good.

I always had a very open relationship with my mother. I could talk to her.

The kids in the neighborhood used to say to me, Ask your mother this, or ask your mother that. It would be a question about sex or boys. They knew she would tell me the truth. She would answer me and I'd tell them.

One particular friend, her parents were older and not open with her. Some of the ideas kids have are really goofy. I can see it now with my own kids. If they don't hear it straight from their parents, then they hear it from the street. It's so twisted up—and they think they know everything. And they know nothing.

So I have that relationship with my daughter now. Open like that.

When Bill and I first got married, I tried working on the third shift. One of the women used to bring me home in the mornings. I would be coming in and Bill would be going out. It was too much.

With Nancy being so young, I wasn't getting enough sleep. I found myself falling asleep during the day. It was just no good, the third shift. So they transferred me to the first.

Day work is so much more normal! And then mother and I found a day care center at the YMCA right up the street from here.

A Play School for Working Mothers they called it.
Nancy loved it and she did really well there. She was three.
My second daughter went to the "Y" too. It was a blessing. I'd put her in in the morning at a little after seven and pick her up at the end of my shift, three-thirty. It cost ten dollars a week then.

I would love for my oldest to go to college. I think she'd really do well but I don't see that for her.
Not because of the money. I would get another job if I had to send her—and I think, in our situation and because of her ability, she'd get scholarships.
She does very well in school but I don't see that for her. I see her following my footsteps—and it frightens me to death—which is: very young, interested in boys, and the boyfriend already, and the hair, and the appearance, and beginning to lose interest in school.
She has no idea what she wants to do or be.
I'd like to see her go to art school. I feel her talent lies in art. She has the potential but she has no confidence in herself. Much like me.
I would have liked to have taught. Been a teacher.
But just the turn of events in my life . . .
Now I think I would have been good at it. I'm good with children, but because of the turn of events in my life it never worked out.
As a youngster, I used to play school but once I got married, with so many things happening, it just escaped me.
What makes me think of it is—I have two girlfriends on my street who are teachers. I'm sort of envious of them. I really would have liked to do that.
My one girlfriend keeps telling me it's never too late, but I don't know.
I don't know if I could even do it today with how different things are, how bad things are. I'm having trouble just sending my children to school.
There are so many problems in the school system today.
I'm considering sending my daughter to Catholic high school.
The tuition is very high but I would do it only because the public school has so many problems.

My husband and I don't have much social life which I hope to rectify soon.
He doesn't drink, which is probably why I was attracted to him.
I'm not a drinker either.
We belong to the social club of Our Lady of Calvary.
Both my daughters went to dancing school there, and there are play activities for them in summer.

That got me involved with the Women's Club. They have social evenings. We enjoy them because our friends go too. Our friends are our neighbors. One of the girls on the block gives a Christmas party for us all every year.
Last year we bought a plastic pool for the girls. A big one, above ground. Four feet. Fifteen around. We cut our vacation short to pay for it. Bill built a little deck.
We're lucky, when I think about it.

Sometimes I get moody like all women do.
I think, "Why do I have to be out working?"
But after I'm home awhile, like if one of the kids gets sick and I have to stay home—or when we're rotating—after a couple of days with the kids I go crazy.
"Why did I think I wanted that?" I ask myself. "I would go crazy staying home all day!"
The grass is always greener until you're there. So, no, I don't think I would quit work. I have now come to the realization that in order to live the way we want to live, and give the kids the things we want to give them, I will be working for the rest of my life. I don't mind.
Not for a common goal.

John Sullivan
Teacher—Writer—Educator

In a boy's mind, you don't think so much of living in a neighborhood with a name like Kensington.
You speak of the streets. Strangers would be those who lived on Cambria Street. The railroad was a border. Frankford Avenue was another.
We never moved beyond those confines too much.
But within them, we seemed to move every few years.
We couldn't pay the rent, so we'd move. There was always this sense of just escaping the rent collector.
I was born on Birch Street near Orleans, south of Allegheny. I haven't been back in years.

My father was a cabinet finisher for Philco. It didn't pay very well. He was active in the unions so he was often laid off.
There was always this sense of being poor. I can still remember one time during the Depression, standing in a long line behind this big wagon, waiting for some kind of a food handout. The shame of it. The anxiety.

My mother never went to school. Born in Scotland, she came here as a girl of fourteen and immediately went to work cleaning for other people. She married young to escape.
My interest in words started when she used to make me read to her. I recall sitting at night reading stories from the magazines. She'd cry, "Buddy! Read it again!"
I'm so ashamed now to think that in my youth I was ashamed of her. I saw only the surface of what she was. When friends came to the house, I was ashamed of her peasant ways. This keeps me humble now.
She couldn't read or write, but she had a canny sense of how to make it. She took good care of us kids. Kept the family together in some bad times. She had a wonderful sense of humor.
She is my ability to accept people now for what they are, my anger at phoniness. Knowing what earthy goodness was, I can talk with plain people, accept them without condescension.

There were nine of us. Three girls and six boys.
We were strangers to each other. What closeness we had was brought about by the simple need to survive. Beyond that, the street was the attraction.
The gang was so important that I had a primary sense of belonging to it, not the family.
I roamed the streets at will. From early morning until late at night. I was self-sufficient. Independent.
Back past the railroad, Trenton Avenue and Somerset, that's where our gang met.
The railroad track was important. It was our playground and a demarcation. It was the place where you were tested as a man.
There was a high trestle. The ground sloped away from it. As a boy, you were challenged to jump the trestle. It was a matter of great courage. I can still feel the fear, standing there, looking down.
The other thing I remember was the trains going down to the shore. The excursion trains. Coming back, the people would toss saltwater taffies out the windows to us.
In the winter we'd steal coal out of the coal cars to take home. It was a battle of wits between us and the train detectives.
To me, a train was something that was always going out of my world instead of passing through.

Thinking back, I remember the sense of excitement and fun of living then.
I told my son a few years ago, *he* was the disadvantaged one.
Kensington was a great place for a boy to grow up in.

We were totally resourceful about our amusement. There was always a game to play. A street game, made up on the spur of the moment. Ever play "Peggy?" Get a broom stick. Break it three feet long. Sharpen one end of a smaller piece. Set it in the street and give it a whack with your broom stick. Try to hit it as far as you can. The other team's fielders try to catch the "peggy" as it flies. It was a game of coordination, excitement, good fun!
Then there was "Kick-the-can." "Half-ball." "Wire-ball."
To play "Wire-ball," you threw a rubber ball against the "telly-pole" wires. If it hit, it counted as a single.
Sometimes we'd earn money hanging around the candy store on Amber Street. In those days, maybe one person in the whole block had a telephone. So a girl would get a telephone call at the candy store. A fellow would call up and say, "I want to talk to Susy Green. She lives at 2130 Birch Street."
The candy store owner would pick one of us to run and get Susy. She'd pay us a nickel. So we hung around the candy store unless we were playing a game.
In those games there was always a keen sense of competition. A ranking of oneself. A choosing of sides.
I was little and heavy so I had a problem.

So many memories come back to me now.
The pretzel baker lived only a block from us. His bakery was in the basement of his house. Late at night, early in the morning, you could see him twisting the pretzel dough, smell the pretzels being baked. They sold for a penny. They were so good!
Another joy we had was to jump in the back of the iceman's wagon and pick up the silver-blue slivers of ice. My chore was to empty the ice pan under our box. I was always a little late and it would be heavy and spill.
The other chore I minded was lifting the heavy ash cans out the basement window to the street.
There was a lot of work for a kid to do. We had a sense of being needed.

Our house was furnished by purchases from door-to-door salesmen. My mother paid a quarter a week for pots, pans, stuffed chairs, sofas, rugs, clothing, pictures, magazines! And every week there would be these men at the door, waiting to collect their quarter or fifty cents.
I would be sent dragging to the door often to say there was no money this week. I dreaded it. The men would get angry. There was never enough money.

One time we were evicted. I don't remember any bitterness about it. It was part of the neighborhood, this sense of the way life was.
You shrugged your shoulders and moved in small circles. Amber Street to Trenton Avenue to Orleans, to Birch. Still seeing the same kids, playing the same games. We were dead enders. Never enough money.
Houses never quite clean from the pervasive layers of industrial dust in the air. But lace curtains at the windows and your front steps washed down every Saturday.
I watched my brothers drift into low-paying jobs inside the neighborhood. At some point in my adolescence, I knew I had to break the circle and get out.

I made up my mind to go to college. My father knew how to hustle the politicians—to use them. They were good to us. Our ward leader always helped with coal in the winter. He got me a Senatorial Scholarship.
College, then, was a matter of riding the trolley car to class. After class, I worked.
I was an artist's model, a seatcover salesman. I worked at night and went to classes in the mornings exhausted.
My mother lived then in Kensington as a widow. My father died at fifty. A stranger to me. I felt no sorrow at his death. Only a stupid, unfeeling coldness. We had nothing in common.
I decided to go into the ministry. I'd become active in a fundamentalist church. But first, in my boyhood, there was the Episcopal Church of Saint John's.
Saint John's had a large cemetery. We'd make love in that cemetery. There was grave robbing, too. Fellows dug up caskets for the gold teeth and rings. The jewelry.
The Sunday School was important. One had a circle of special Sunday friends.
I sang in the church choir. I loved the Episcopal prayer book. Beautiful seventeenth century English prose.
I was convinced I should become a preacher at nineteen. I preached at a church in Germantown on weekends. A callow adolescent at the pulpit mouthing empty phrases.
Then I went into the service, and in coming back to finish college, I realized I'd make a better teacher.
I had a teacher, Miss Devlin, who cared about the English language. She made me care too. I wanted to talk the way she did.
I started teaching English at Kensington High School, still going to college at night to get my Master's Degree—my Doctorate.

Pushing. Pushing.
One time my mother said to me, "John, how long you been going to college?"
I said, "Sixteen years, mom."
She shook her head and said, "I thought school got finished in four."

After ten years at Kensington High School, I became a department chairman.
I got a fellowship to study educational ideas in Chicago. The school superintendent was so impressed with the report I wrote, he offered to make me principal of the junior high.
Now I teach at the university, in the school of education.
Do a lot of writing of my own. Textbooks mostly, on the teaching of English in the schools.

Once or twice a year the family gets together. We talk about the old days. Memories.
Refreshments at the gathering are always predictable.
Beer and cold cuts.
I stay an hour and leave, saying to myself, they are part of me.
My family. That's my flesh and blood.
But I wonder how I happened to be different.

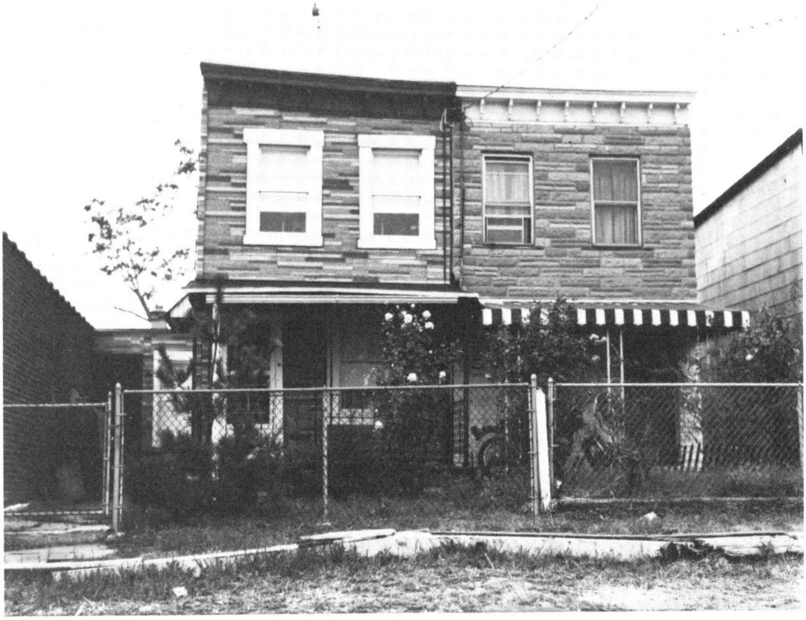

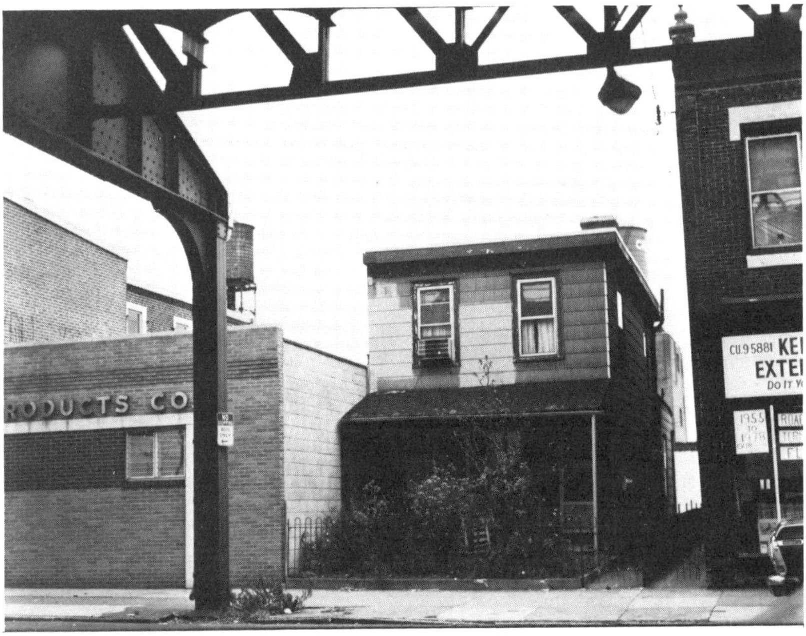
RODUCTS CO
CU.9 5881

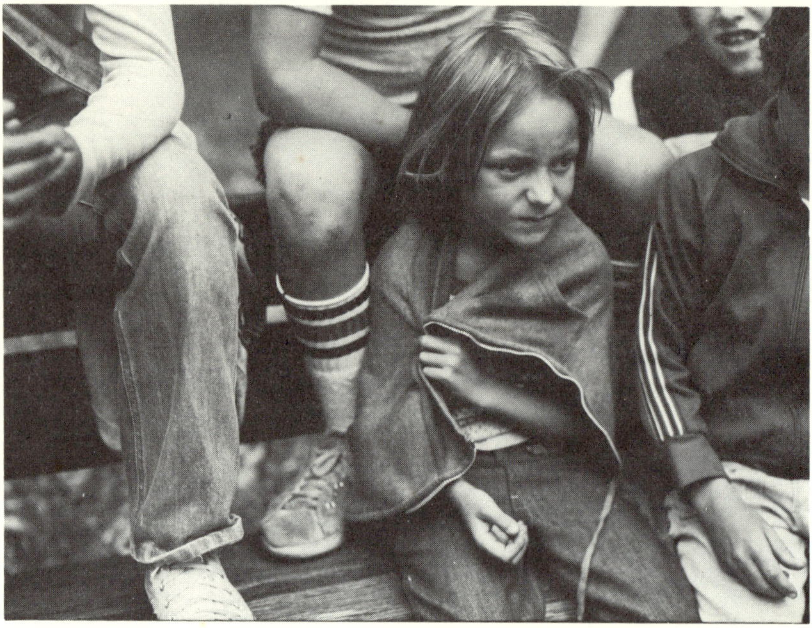

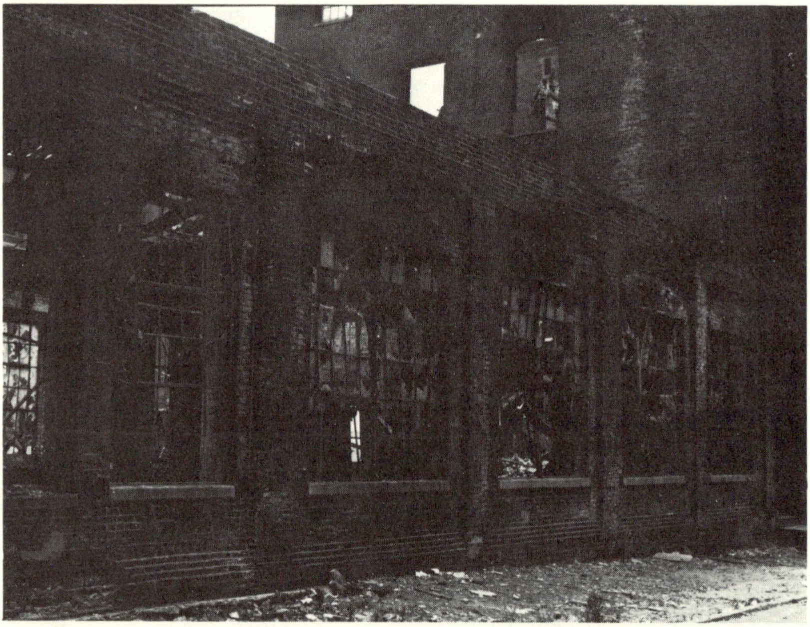